HOW T
SUCCESSFU

ALISON HARDINGHA
Worcestershire, and stu
Margaret Hall, Oxford. She trained as a teacher and
worked in teaching before moving on to educational
psychology, including family therapy and assessment of
children. She now works in industry, for a consultancy
which specializes in advising organizations about human
factors in information systems.

Overcoming Common Problems Series

The ABC of Eating
Coping with anorexia, bulimia and
compulsive eating
JOY MELVILLE

An A–Z of Alternative Medicine
BRENT Q. HAFEN AND KATHRYN J.
FRANDSEN

Arthritis
Is your suffering really necessary?
DR WILLIAM FOX

Birth Over Thirty
SHEILA KITZINGER

Body Language
How to read others' thoughts by their gestures
ALLAN PEASE

Calm Down
How to cope with frustration and anger
DR PAUL HAUCK

Comfort for Depression
JANET HORWOOD

Common Childhood Illnesses
DR PATRICIA GILBERT

Complete Public Speaker
GYLES BRANDRETH

Coping with Depression and Elation
DR PATRICK McKEON

Coping Successfully with Your Child's Asthma
DR PAUL CARSON

**Coping Successfully with Your Child's Skin
Problems**
DR PAUL CARSON

**Coping Successfully with Your Hyperactive
Child**
DR PAUL CARSON

Curing Arthritis Cookbook
MARGARET HILLS

Curing Arthritis – The Drug-free Way
MARGARET HILLS

Curing Illness – The Drug-free Way
MARGARET HILLS

Depression
DR PAUL HAUCK

Divorce and Separation
ANGELA WILLANS

The Epilepsy Handbook
SHELAGH McGOVERN

Everything You Need to Know about Adoption
MAGGIE JONES

**Everything You Need to Know about Contact
Lenses**
DR ROBERT YOUNGSON

**Everything You Need to Know about Your
Eyes**
DR ROBERT YOUNGSON

**Everything You Need to Know about the
Pill**
WENDY COOPER AND TOM SMITH

Everything You Need to Know about Shingles
DR ROBERT YOUNGSON

Family First Aid and Emergency Handbook
DR ANDREW STANWAY

Fears and Phobias
What they are and how to overcome them
DR TONY WHITEHEAD

Feverfew
A traditional herbal remedy for migraine and
arthritis
DR STEWART JOHNSON

Fight Your Phobia and Win
DAVID LEWIS

Flying Without Fear
TESSA DUCKWORTH AND DAVID
MILLER

Overcoming Common Problems Series

Goodbye Backache
DR DAVID IMRIE WITH COLLEEN
DIMSON

Good Publicity Guide
REGINALD PEPLOW

Helping Children Cope with Grief
ROSEMARY WELLS

How to Be Your Own Best Friend
DR PAUL HAUCK

How to Control your Drinking
DRS W. MILLER AND R. MUNOZ

How to Cope with Stress
DR PETER TYRER

How to Cope with your Child's Allergies
DR PAUL CARSON

How to Cope with your Nerves
DR TONY LAKE

How to Cope with Tinnitus and Hearing Loss
DR ROBERT YOUNGSON

How to Do What You Want to Do
DR PAUL HAUCK

How to Enjoy Your Old Age
DR B. F. SKINNER AND M. E.
VAUGHAN

How to Improve Your Confidence
DR KENNETH HAMBLY

How to Interview and Be Interviewed
MICHELE BROWN AND
GYLES BRANDRETH

How to Love and be Loved
DR PAUL HAUCK

How to Say No to Alcohol
KEITH McNEILL

How to Sleep Better
DR PETER TYRER

How to Stand up for Yourself
DR PAUL HAUCK

How to Start a Conversation and Make Friends
DON GABOR

How to Stop Feeling Guilty
DR VERNON COLEMAN

How to Stop Smoking
GEORGE TARGET

How to Stop Taking Tranquillisers
DR PETER TYRER

If Your Child is Diabetic
JOANNE ELLIOTT

Jealousy
DR PAUL HAUCK

Learning to Live with Multiple Sclerosis
DR ROBERT POVEY, ROBIN DOWIE
AND GILLIAN PRETT

Living with Grief
DR TONY LAKE

Living Through Personal Crisis
ANN KAISER STEARNS

Living with High Blood Pressure
DR TOM SMITH

Loneliness
DR TONY LAKE

Making Marriage Work
DR PAUL HAUCK

Making the Most of Loving
GILL COX AND SHEILA DAINOW

Making the Most of Middle Age
DR BRICE PITT

Making the Most of Yourself
GILL COX AND SHEILA DAINOW

Overcoming Common Problems Series

Overcoming Common Problems

HOW TO MAKE
SUCCESSFUL DECISIONS

Alison Hardingham

SHELDON PRESS
LONDON

First published in Great Britain in 1988 by
Sheldon Press, SPCK, Marylebone Road, London NW1 4DU

Copyright © Alison Hardingham 1988

All rights reserved. No part of this book may be reproduced
or transmitted in any form or by any means, electronic or
mechanical, including photocopying, recording, or by any
information storage and retrieval system, without permission
in writing from the publisher.

British Library Cataloguing in Publication Data

Hardingham, Alison,
    How to make successful decisions. ——
    (Overcoming common problems).
    1. Decision making
    I. Title   II. Series
    153.8'3

    ISBN 0–85969–576–X

Photoset by Deltatype Ltd, Ellesmere Port, Cheshire
Printed in Great Britain by Richard Clay Ltd, Bungay, Suffolk

Contents

Introduction

The ability to make effective decisions is a fundamental requirement for both professional success and personal happiness. An
effective decision is one which brings about, more or less, the
state of affairs you were hoping for. More than that, an effective
decision can result in surprising but welcome changes to your
life. An ineffective decision, in contrast, has either little or the
wrong effect.

Although effective decision-making is so essential to all areas
of our lives, from career choices through marriage to the
education and upbringing of our children, we spend relatively
little time considering how to go about it, and indeed often little
time actually carrying it out. This book aims to redress the
balance. It aims firstly to stimulate interest in making decisions,
so that the reader begins to see decision-making as something
important which deserves his or her full attention. Secondly, the
book unfolds, chapter by chapter, a strategy for making
decisions which will enable the decision-maker to become more
effective.

Ineffective decision-makers are fearful of taking charge of
their lives. They evade and side-step. Perhaps because they have
never realized the importance of sound decision-making, they
find the work involved tedious and skip it whenever they can.

Effective decision-makers, on the other hand, have a spring in
their step. They approach each decision with confidence, alert-
ness, and enthusiasm. They know how to go about weighing up
the pros and cons, how to meet deadlines, and how to consult
others for advice. In addition, they find making decisions fun.
They take it seriously, but they enjoy the challenge.

There is a school of thought which teaches that for most
important characteristics people are either born with them or
without them. There is little we can do to change what we are.
This school of thought would say that either you are an effective
decision-maker or you are not. This book takes the opposite

view. It is based on the belief that most people can change their decision-making habits, if they wish, just as they can change their daily routine or their diet. We can learn skills which make us effective decision-makers and we can apply a practical technique.

So this book is for anyone who wants to improve their decision-making, be it at school, at home or at work. The approach described here is not complex or intellectually demanding. It is, on the whole, applied common-sense.

The book was written with busy people in mind. We often dismiss a new activity or exercise as too time-consuming. Sometimes this is just an excuse, but often we are genuinely too harassed and preoccupied to include yet another new element in our lives. So the approach described in this book is as simple as it can be. It does not require you to drop everything and concentrate on your decision-making. That would be counter-productive. It does not require you to change your lifestyle. It provides a short series of steps which can be fitted into your standard routine, and which will ensure that your decision-making rests on solid foundations. There are also many suggestions about how to use time more efficiently when making decisions. In the end the approach put forward in the pages which follow should save you time.

The book includes many examples of decisions to illustrate the relevance of the approach it advocates. These examples cover a variety of decisions and of people making them. They are drawn from situations I have been involved in personally, or have studied in the course of my work as educational and occupational psychologist. The people I describe are fictional, but the decision-making patterns are the ones which I have encountered, in various forms, over and over again. Through my work and my personal experiences I have become convinced that effective decision-making is fundamental to full enjoyment of life, and that the means to achieve it are within the reach of all of us.

1

Why Decisions Can Be Good For You

Common attitudes to making decisions

I wonder how often you have heard someone say, with irritation, despair, resignation or even fear, 'I've got to come to a decision'. Rarely is it said with enthusiasm or pleasure. People have been known to live in misery and uncertainty for years rather than make a decision. The very words we use to talk about making decisions reveal how unpleasant we find them. We describe them as hard or even impossible, and talk in terms of facing up to or agonizing over a decision.

The strategies we adopt to minimize our contact with these unpleasant and frightening entities are many and varied. We pretend they are not really there—the 'Of course, there's only one real option' approach. We avoid them—the 'I'm far too busy to waste time agonizing over that' approach. We put them off—the 'Don't cross that bridge until you come to it' approach. We hand them over to someone else, fast—the 'My husband/wife/son deals with all the money matters' approach.

Hiding from a frightening decision

Susie Jeffreys hid from a decision for many months. She discovered her husband was having an affair which he had no intention of finishing. In fact, he was becoming steadily more committed to his mistress and less committed to Susie and their small daughter. Susie knew that she would have to make up her mind whether to leave him or not.

She avoided even thinking about this decision. She organized an extremely busy social life for herself and her daughter. She took up a correspondence course in English literature. She threw herself into renovating their house. All of these activities can be seen as avoidance strategies. The consequences of this avoidance were severe both for her and her daughter. Her health deteriorated. Her little girl became uncertain and rebellious, in turns.

3

Whenever her family or friends tried to talk to Susie about the decision she had to make, she burst into tears. She could talk intelligently and articulately about her daughter, the house, even the affair, but not about the decision.

After eighteen months of avoidance, Susie decided to leave her husband. She now lives alone with her daughter. Both she and her child are physically healthier and more sure of themselves. They have left purgatory and started on the path to a new life.

The important point in this example is that Susie chose sickness, stress and pain for herself and her daughter for eighteen months rather than take a decision. Looked at coldly and objectively, such behaviour seems crazy. But in fact Susie was not crazy, just frightened. She saw the decision as an abyss opening up before her, not as the first rung of a ladder to better times.

Leaving a difficult decision to chance

It is not only fear which makes us avoid decisions. Laziness comes into it, too. If we know that there is a decision we should make which will require a lot of hard thinking and investigation of alternatives, we often put it off until finally some event or person beyond our control makes the decision for us. An analogy will make clear how much we can lose if we take this approach.

Choice, not Chance. Imagine you are sitting in a restaurant. The waiter arrives and hands you the menu. What are you feeling at this point? Perhaps interest, excitement; above all, you are looking forward to seeing the range of dishes you have to choose from. Few people would try to evade this pleasant choice. You don't see many people tossing a coin as they inspect the menu. You would not dream of closing your eyes and sticking a pin in the menu. You would feel you had lost out if someone else chose for you, or if only one of the dishes was available.

A decision can be seen as a menu. Different possibilities for your life are laid out before you. You are the one to choose. If you don't choose yourself, if you don't devote your attention to the decision as you would to a menu, then you will lose out.

Reasons for common attitudes to making decisions

We can explore the differences between choosing a dish from a menu and making an important decision to discover why a menu fills us with eager anticipation while an imminent decision provokes dread and ultimately avoidance.

Clearly the consequences are on different scales. The worst consequences of a poor choice from a menu are a meal we don't enjoy, a bill we can't afford to pay, or a stomach upset. The best consequence is simply an enjoyable evening. The consequences of an important decision may, on the other hand, affect your happiness or success for years to come.

How strange that we should devote such close attention to a menu, then, while ignoring and avoiding decisions of consequence. But this pattern of behaviour is in fact a familiar one. We spend a lot of time in straightforward activities, where success is likely and the penalties of failure slight, while we avoid difficult tasks with high potential costs and benefits.

The timescales of a menu-choice and an important decision are of course very different. Most menus can be read thoroughly in a few minutes. Few important decisions can be dismissed even in a few hours. We find it difficult to sustain our concentration and focus on the matter in hand. It is easier to rush the decision, and then forget about it.

Another fundamental difference between a menu-choice and an important decision is the amount of information you need for each. When you look at a menu, you already know most of what you need to make a good choice. If there are any dishes you do not recognize, a waiter can describe them to you readily. If you have to make a decision such as whether to buy a particular house there are many and varied questions which need to be researched and answered before you are in a position to decide. Small wonder that we find this sort of decision daunting!

No one will criticize your choice of meal in a restaurant. The consequences affect only you, providing you are paying the bill. No one else is in a position to pass judgement on you, since you are the best judge of your own taste. When it comes to making decisions, however, we frequently come under fire from our friends, family and neighbours. 'Back-seat decision-makers' abound. We may be told 'Everything would have been fine if you hadn't decided to change your solicitor/take a part-time job/send your son to public school'. This kind of comment is very difficult to cope with, particularly since it could be true. It is hardly surprising that we try to avoid making decisions which could let us in for such criticisms.

A positive approach to making decisions

It is clear that we have good reason to try to avoid making decisions, in the sense that we are correct in regarding the process as difficult and risky. Yet it is also clear that we need to overcome the problems that decisions pose not by evading the issue but by mastering effective decision-making. This book is about seeing decisions as essential ladders to where we want to be, not yawning chasms to swallow us up. It is about making decisions into opportunities, not ogres.

Every time you make a choice, you are asserting your individuality and power. You are actively taking charge of your life and determining its course, rather than passively awaiting the pushes and shoves of fate. Even apparently trivial, commonplace decisions, such as choosing what to cook for dinner, how to arrange the furniture, or which channel to watch on TV, are tiny assertions of freedom. Even these decisions offer us a chance for change and development.

This book is not primarily concerned with everyday decisions, although the ideas developed in it can be applied to minor decisions as well as major. It focuses on the most frightening decisions of all, those decisions whose effects will play a large part in shaping the rest of your life. These are the decisions which might make you reach for one of those executive toys, where a steel ball hangs suspended on a wire between several magnetic plates. We flick the ball and let its random jerks determine our choice, another denial of responsibility, another missed opportunity to exercise power over our lives.

Hopefully, once you have read this book, you will restrict the use of these toys to choices such as whether to have a bath now or

wait until after the 9 o'clock news. You will be neither irritated nor frightened at the prospect of making a decision, since you will have at your disposal a positive strategy for making the most of every decision that comes your way.

Discovering your own attitude: the first exercise

How can you tell whether your own attitude to making decisions is based on fear and avoidance, or on assertiveness and determination? Naturally your attitude may vary from one decision to another. You may be very comfortable and confident with decisions in one sphere, troubled and insecure about decisions in another. In many marriages, for example, the husband will make important decisions as a matter of course at work, but rely entirely on his wife to make the decisions about their social life, their holidays, even their children.

So it is useful to consider your own decision-making pattern. As you read this, you will be aware that you have already made, or had made for you, many critical decisions. You have been educated within a particular system, you may be married or divorced, you may have children, you live in a particular part of the country with a particular daily routine.

One of the themes of this book is the importance of organized thinking in making reasoned decisions. I have come to regard pen and paper as an invaluable tool for organized thinking, so many of the exercises I suggest in this book involve writing. It is helpful to see suggestions, ideas, arguments, pictures, written or drawn before you. Writing things down helps you to become separate from your ideas and to judge them with a degree of objectivity. It also stops you pretending to yourself that you have 'already thought of dozens of reasons why it isn't a good idea'. How many dozens? Write them down and find out.

The first exercise in this book, then, involves pen and paper. Write down five major decisions that have been made which affected your life. For each decision write down who made it. Now write down who really made it! Then write down who was most qualified to make it. Here are some examples.

1	*(Decision)*	Family move to London
	(Who made it?)	My father
	(Who really made it?)	My father's boss
	(Who was most qualified to make it?)	My mother
2	*(Decision)*	I go to Eton
	(Who made it?)	My father
	(Who really made it?)	My father
	(Who was most qualified to make it?)	My mother
3	*(Decision)*	I go to Cambridge
	(Who made it?)	Me
	(Who really made it?)	My house-master
	(Who was most qualified to make it?)	My house-master
4	*(Decision)*	I marry Jane
	(Who made it?)	Me
	(Who really made it?)	Jane
	(Who was most qualified to make it?)	Jane's parents
5	*(Decision)*	We move to Dorset
	(Who made it?)	Jane
	(Who really made it?)	Jane
	(Who was most qualified to make it?)	?

Don't spend too long on this. Often it is impossible to work out who was best qualified to make a decision, especially if you are still close to that decision in time.

The list probably demonstrates three things. First, many decisions which were important for you were not made by you. Secondly, the real decision-makers are often behind-the-scenes people, who may never tell anyone to do anything overtly, but who manoeuvre them into a choice nevertheless. Thirdly, it is extremely difficult to judge who is most qualified to make a given decision, even with the benefit of hindsight.

All these three things point to the importance of your taking charge of making decisions. You do not want, I presume, to be manipulated. Neither do you want second-best decisions to be made about your own, and one and only, life. So, rather than hand over responsibility, explicitly or implicitly, to someone else, whose competence to make such a decision will more often than not be open to doubt, you must make the decision yourself. Of course, you will take advice. We shall discuss this later. Having gathered as much information as you need, however, you will choose. Then it will be your own mistakes that you live with, and every mistake will help you improve your decision-making ability.

That is not to say you will do everything your own way, without involving other people. Some of the best decisions are made by couples who have learnt to work together to achieve a goal—on no account to be confused with committees, who have learnt to work together to achieve nothing. The reins are in your hands, but they can be in more than one pair of hands at once. We shall talk about joint or team decisions in Chapter Eight. For now, I want to stress your own importance. It's your life—you are the one to make or mar it.

Discover your own attitude: the second exercise

The first exercise may have enlightened you about your general attitude to decisions. This exercise is concerned with determining your attitude to any particular decision.

Think of a decision you must make in the near future. (If you can't think of one, that probably tells you a great deal! Since the normal course of our lives imposes a whole series of decisions upon us, if you can't think of one which is coming up it suggests that either someone else is making the decisions for you or you aren't practised at recognizing decisions for what they are. In either case, read on!) Write the decision down. Now tick the word in each of the word-pairs below that best describes how you felt as you wrote the decision.

> keen/indifferent
> interested/bored
> hopeful/despairing
> calm/anxious
> determined/wavering

If most of your ticks were for the second word in a pair, your attitude is negative and you probably won't be able to make that decision effectively. If most of your ticks were for the first words, you are well set to begin on a bit of effective decision-making.

Effective decisions when you don't feel effective. You have already taken the first step to ensuring that your fear or irritation does not compromise your decision-making. You have recognized your attitude. You have recognized that you don't feel effective. You will be alerted to your own desire to avoid or rush the decision.

You cannot change your attitude by an act of will. But you can engage in effective decision-making *despite* your attitude. The steps outlined in the remaining chapters of this book can be followed whatever your attitude. They are practical. They will be harder to follow if you do not enjoy making decisions, but more necessary. In addition, as you make more and more decisions using the approach described in this book, your attitude will change in consequence. Because you will have a strategy for tackling decisions, you will be less frightened. Because you will have seen how the effectiveness of your decision-making affects your life, you will be less bored.

For the very fearful, however, here is just one exercise designed to make starting on that process a little easier.

Starting to change your attitude: the first exercise

Decision-making is important but not life-threatening. Write down one good decision you have made, and one disastrous one. Then list the consequences of each. Try and choose decisions which you made sufficiently long ago to know now of just about all the consequences.

Here is an example.
    A good decision:
—to change my job from teaching to accountancy.
    Consequences
—more interesting work, good social life attached, much more

money, travelling rather a chore, nights away from home, less security, more status, less time for my children, afford nice house, nice holidays.

A bad decision:

—to move to Newcastle

Consequences

—miss our friends, schools bad, cannot afford to move back South into a nice house, cold weather, cat run over.

The first point is that you will have already noticed that it is virtually impossible to guarantee you know all the consequences of a decision. Even if you put down decisions you made decades ago, you will have realized that they may even have effects on your future life, as yet unanticipated. So we can learn from this that there is no such thing as the best decision (or the worst decision). Do not spend any time at all looking for the best decision. Just spend whatever time is available on making a competent one. You would have to have a crystal ball to predict everything your decision will entail. If you develop the skill of reasonably quick, reasonably competent decision-making, however, on the whole your life will be more the way you want it.

The second point which follows from the exercise is that, self-evidently, even your bad decision was not the end of the world. Probably even as you wrote it you were thinking that it was not so bad after all, that you had just about recovered, that if you hadn't made it you would never have met John/seen Austria/been able to laugh at misfortune, whatever. People do die from decisions, of course. All the time. But you are even more likely to die from failing to make a decision.

So it is unlikely that single, or even a series of, bad decisions will ruin your life. On the other hand, if you practise the skills and attitudes discussed in this book, the quality of your life may be enhanced.

2

The Hidden Decisions:
Asking the Right Question

Decision frames

This chapter is about spotting the decisions you make without thinking before you realize you've done it. It is also about ensuring that you are making real decisions rather than pretend ones.

Often the way you phrase or 'frame' your decision rules out some of the good alternatives. It may rule out the most attractive alternative.

Let me give you an example. Let us suppose that I am trying to decide whether to leave my job or not. I have just been offered a promotion. I had, however, been thinking of moving on, to a bigger company which would offer me a wider variety of work. I frame my decision as the following:

'Shall I leave my job or stay?'
An alternative way of framing this decision will be:
'When shall I leave my job?'

Immediately, the picture changes. It is rather like an ambiguous drawing where, once you have been given the key, all the pieces appear to move and take on a new shape. If I think of the decision in terms of when, rather than if, I should change jobs, I begin to examine the advantages and disadvantages of different time-scales. I may decide now is the wrong time in any event.

Can you 're-frame' these decisions?

1. Shall I buy a dog?
2. Shall we have my Mother to live with us or not?
3. Shall I tell my next-door neighbour his stereo keeps us awake?
4. Shall I sack my cleaning lady or just 'forget' to give her a payrise?

Here are some suggested re-framings. They are not the only ones by any means.

1. Do I want a pet?
   What kind of pet do I want?
2. What can we do to ensure Mother is safe and not too lonely now that Father has died?
3. What can I do to stop the next-door neighbour playing his stereo loud after midnight?
4. How can I make sure the house is kept clean?

You can see from the reframings suggested above that many decisions are prematurely framed as 'either/or' choices and that 'How?' and 'What?' questions are often a better first step to making a decision. They offer more scope and flexibility. They encourage us to examine what exactly it is that we want to achieve.

Offering choice where the range of choice is defined is a powerful way of limiting people's freedom whilst appearing to be libertarian. You say to your children, 'Would you like to go to bed before the comedy show or after?' Then they may overlook to raise the issue of whether to go to bed at your request at all. The wife says to her husband, 'If you're too tired to arrange the ferry bookings, I'll do it.' Now if he wants to avoid making the ferry bookings, he appears to be weak. Perhaps he is not tired *and* he does not intend to arrange them. He may be intending to put his foot down and tell his wife that she should be arranging the holiday plans. His wife is trying to preclude that possibility.

Many books have been, and could be, written on how to challenge this kind of manipulation coming from others. I want to stress here that we also limit our own freedom and range of choice by imposing artificial choices on ourselves. We do it because we are too lazy or too frightened to investigate the real choices. Yet by doing it we build a cage around ourselves, bar by bar. It doesn't just keep strange and unwelcome realities out; it hems us in.

So as soon as you have become aware of a decision that you must make, write it down. Then actively search for other ways of putting it, other options you have not thought of, and examine the question closely for its hidden assumptions. Some of them are no doubt justified; if they are, nothing is lost by subjecting them to scrutiny. If they are unjustified, exposing them will give you more freedom of choice.

In the example discussed at the beginning of this chapter, where I framed my decision as *either* to leave my job *or* to take the promotion, my choice may be guided by a reluctance not to let down my employers. I then have to ask myself, however, whether these feelings of loyalty are appropriate, and whether I am being motivated by a desire to avoid conflict.

Opening decisions up

An essential step towards framing your decisions properly is taking a wide view of them in the beginning. Do not treat a decision in isolation, but think of it in context. Here is a list of questions to ask yourself about any particular decision to 'open it up'.

What has brought me to the point of making this decision?
Does it entail making any other decisions first?
Will it result in any further decisions?
Is this decision intended to overcome a problem?
If so, are there any other ways of overcoming the problem?
Who will be affected by this decision?
What changes will there be to my life as a result of making this decision?
Do I feel ready to make this decision?
Do I feel happy about making this decision?
Why am I making this decision now?
Why haven't I made this decision before?
Have I got a free choice?
If not, in what ways is my choice limited?

It is quite fun and also informative to pretend to be a perverse and inquisitive questioner of your own decisions. Here is an example of how an imagined conversation might go.

You: 'I'm trying to decide whether to buy a new car.'
Imaginary inquisitor: 'Why?'

14

'Because I had a big bill last MOT.'

'You'll have an even bigger bill if you buy a new car.'

'Yes, but I can plan for that.'

'So plan for your next MOT bill. Why are you *really* considering buying a new car?'

'I'm bored with the old one.'

'Can you afford to be that bored? . . .'

and so on, until you give up or suddenly realize you shouldn't be making that decision after all!

It is at this early stage that you should try to be as imaginative as possible about the decision you think you have to make. Avoid either putting yourself or letting other people put you in a decision-making strait-jacket. Most thirteen-year-olds, for example, are given a very limited choice in their decisions on which exam subjects to take. The choice is restricted by school timetabling and staffing. In this decision, as in all others of importance, the first selection should ignore the constraints. Draw up the ideal set of subjects. Then you can choose where to make compromises, and explore possibilities for unusual combinations of subjects: private tutoring, lessons during lunchhours, correspondence courses, and so on.

Narrowing decisions down

It is sometimes necessary to do the opposite of opening a decision up. Some decisions are put in such a universal frame that they impose a sort of paralysis on anyone who tries to tackle them. Then it is necessary to narrow the decision down.

An example of a decision which is framed too broadly for action is the 'What shall I do with my life?' dilemma. As a topic to ponder over this is an excellent question. As the lead-in to effective decision-making, it is a non-starter. If you find yourself continually asking yourself, and others, this kind of question, you need at some point to sharpen your focus. 'What shall I do with my life?' can be sharpened in many different ways. Here are some examples.

What shall I do with the next year? (*narrowing the time-frame*)
What shall I do next in my career? (*narrowing the subject-frame*)

Am I content with life as it is? (*narrowing the thought-frame*)

At an early stage of making a major decision it is helpful to play with your focus on the decision. Open the decision up one day, to discover all its implications and ramifications. Narrow it down another until it leads to a clear choice between one course of action and another.

Deceptive decisions

Playing with your focus on a decision should help you to avoid being misled by the true meaning of a decision you suddenly find yourself having to make. Sometimes what appears to be a central decision is in fact a red herring, a sidetrack, from something of much more fundamental importance to your life. Occasionally we find ourselves plunging with relief into decisions like these, which represent escape from problems which are almost too big to face. Preoccupation with decisions about what to wear, or eat, and continuous fretting over minor domestic matters, are characteristic of this frame of mind. But even decisions which are serious and important in their own right can serve a deceptive purpose.

A little decision which hid a big one. I was consulted recently by a lady with a one-year old son. I shall call her Harriet. She told me that she was trying to decide whether to send her son to a crèche full-time in a few months. She had to make the decision in a hurry, Harriet told me, because the other parents who were setting up the crèche wanted a definite answer as soon as possible. She simply wanted to know, from me, at what age a child would benefit and not suffer from spending his day in a small group of children of similar age, looked after by one or two adults.

I gave her a quick answer, that in my opinion two and a half was the youngest age at which a child could cope with that sort of arrangement, since it would mean putting him into social situations for long periods most days without his parents.

I was surprised that Harriet had asked me this question. I knew that she had very much wanted her son and had been looking forward to bringing him up. She had given up teaching even before the child had been conceived because she wanted to devote herself to her family. It was curious that she should now be preoccupied with whether to pack the child off to a crèche five days a week.

On inquiring further, I discovered that this decision was just the tip of an iceberg. Harriet's relationship with her father had deteriorated drastically in the last two months. Her contact with him was infrequent and very distressing when it occurred. For the sake of her own peace of mind, Harriet had some fundamental decisions to make about the future of her relationship with her father and about what he could reasonably expect of her and she of him.

These underlying stresses, which she did not feel able to resolve, had made her look for an escape. Returning to work, conforming to the two-income-plus-child-care philosophy of the set she now lived amongst, preoccupying herself with decisions she could handle, were her ways of coping.

Yet the decision about child-care for her son could not sensibly be made until she had resolved the fundamental questions. Given there was a risk to her son's happiness in putting him into the crèche too early, Harriet had to decide how important it was to her to return to work. To do that, she had to decide whether that was the best way to cope with the conflict with her father. The decisions were nested inside each other, like a set of Russian dolls. They had to be unpacked, and then put together again in the right order, the innermost decision first, for the last decision to be made with confidence.

If Harriet had gone ahead with the decision on daytime care for her son without making the necessary decisions about her relationship with her own father first, there would have been two main dangers. Firstly, she and her son would have been committed to a way of life without Harriet's fully understanding why she had chosen it. She would be less able to consider the pros and cons of that way of life with insight and rationality. Secondly, Harriet might never have resolved the conflict with her father. Then she would find herself making more decisions for reasons she could not acknowledge, even to herself, and more of her life would be determined by a hidden source of unease and distress.

An easy decision which hid a difficult one. Pete was choosing a new car. He had just been promoted and he could afford to treat himself. He liked sports cars. His girl-friend was expecting their first child in a couple of months. They had been living together for several years, and the decision to have a child had appeared to be a joint one. She was enthusiastic about Pete's success at work, and delighted that he could afford a new car. He had been working very hard over the previous year and deserved a reward.

It didn't take Pete long to make up his mind. He bought a two-seater convertible. He had liked that particular car for a long time and he was delighted with it. He didn't ask himself why he had chosen a car which his pregnant girl-friend could only drive with difficulty and in which he could never drive his girl-friend and child. It was just a decision about a car.

In fact, it was anything but a decision about a car. It was a decision about priorities. Without giving it even a moment's conscious thought, Pete had decided his first priority was to please himself. He had begun to define limits to his commitment to his girl-friend and their child-to-be.

Had he paused to consider whether he was prepared to change in response to the birth of his child, he would have had some difficult decisions to make. He had always thought of himself as a kind man, inclined to be rather put upon by more forceful personalities. If you had pressed him, he would have said he was on the unselfish side. Yet he had just made a choice which was seriously selfish.

Pete would have laughed if you had suggested there was anything 'behind' his decision to buy a sports car. Yet as the months went by, he made more and more easy decisions, both minor and major, which distanced him from his girl-friend. He decided to accept a further promotion which involved frequent visits abroad. He started to go out more in the evenings with the crowd from work. He decided not to ask any friends from work to their house-warming party. Pete's girl-friend never met the secretary he eventually left her for.

Right up to the point of no return, Pete kept his decision-making focus deliberately narrow. He never wanted to make the difficult decision, whether he was going to stay with his girl-friend and child or leave. Instead, he made a series of easy decisions which finally made the difficult decision for him.

The Argument for Honest Decision-Making

Fatalists argue that there is no point in honest decision-making, which is essentially what I have been advocating so far in this chapter. They maintain that the course your life takes is determined, in all respects which matter, by actions, motivations and events over which we have no conscious control.

A religious fatalist credits God with the only true control. A behaviourist fatalist claims early conditioning determines all our actions by the time we are adult. A biological fatalist attributes it all to our genetic inheritance. Such views suggest that decision-making is never anything more than the rationalization of actions which have already been decided. In fact, decisions are an illusion with which we intelligent puppets console ourselves.

Obviously I do not hold this view. The choice between fatalism and a more hopeful view of human choice is, however, a personal and essentially ideological one. I cannot prove that we can exert real control over our lives.

In fact, though, no-one lives as a true fatalist would, however fatalistic he may claim to be. Certainly in day-to-day matters we all assume that the laws of cause and effect apply. We look before we cross the road. We eat. We choose what to wear. We argue with each other, hope, and are disappointed.

Paradoxically, people who claim to be fatalistic reserve the expression of their fatalism for the really important decisions in their lives. I have heard people resign themselves to appallingly unhappy marriages, serious physical pain, and deep disappointment in their children with fatalistic comments such as 'It's God's will' or 'That's life'. By reacting like this, they guarantee that they will never effect an improvement in their own lives, they will never be agents of change for themselves and those they care about. They confirm their own belief that there is no point in struggling against Fate, however they may choose to define it. And therein lies the fatalist fallacy. If you behave fatalistically, you are sure to lose any control over your life which you might have had.

The plot thickens when we consider why some people are inclined to react in this way. It seems likely that we are inclined to give up because we have tried to exert control and failed. Children who have had their hopes disappointed and their ambitions thwarted by their parents often turn into fatalistic adults. Elderly people whose spouse has died turn towards fatalism. Yet such a response to failure precludes for ever the possibility of future success.

There is another type of fatalism, the kind which is adopted to avoid responsibility. This is the person whose constant complaint is 'I couldn't help it. That's the way I'm made.' I do not think such people are interested in effective decision-making. They are already experts in effective manipulation. Their apparent plea of impotence in fact ensures that they can always do just as they want without taking the feelings and needs of others into account and without taking any responsibility for behaving selfishly.

We are all a little fatalistic at times. But even when we feel out of control, the only way to get back in control is to practise honest, and effective, decision-making.

Wasting and saving time

Making sure your decisions are framed properly and playing with your decision-making focus are activities which take time. In the early stages of making a decision, you will probably be anxious to get on with it, reluctant to spend time on what appear to be luxuries. Yet these early activities are the most important. You will waste far more time if you go ahead to make and perhaps even implement an inappropriate decision.

Be honest with yourself. If you find yourself saying 'I haven't time for all this', are you sure you're not saying 'I don't want to do this'? And if you don't want to practise honest decision-making, maybe you should ask yourself why.

3

The Worst Bit:
Collecting Information

Chapter Two dealt with asking the right question. Asking the right question is a good beginning, but the next step is tricky. As soon as you have formulated a question, answers spring to mind. People often behave as if it were a problem to find answers to the questions their life poses: the problem in fact is to hold superficial answers at bay while you collect enough information to come up with a good answer.

Learning to live with uncertainty

We dislike uncertainty in our lives. A question represents unfinished business; a decision to be made is like an open door letting in a draught. We rush to shut the door, relieved as it slams, almost no matter what the outcome.

This is why I have called this chapter 'the worst bit'. All the time you are collecting information to make your decision, you are in the draught from that open door. You cannot be sure what will happen, you cannot prepare yourself yet for the outcome, you cannot begin to 'look on the bright side' because you don't know what to look on the bright side of.

Learning to live with uncertainty is unfortunately a prerequisite for making competent decisions. Unless you can suspend judgement, your information-gathering will be biased and curtailed. If you decide on the answer before you know as many of the facts as you can, you will be prejudicing your own decisions.

Now it is clearly not possible to set aside all your preformed ideas and preferences which are relevant to the decision you must make. None of us can become a blank slate at will, none of us can weigh up the evidence with total impartiality. Indeed, since it is our life we are making decisions about, it is important that we take our gut feelings, however unreasonable, into account. What is possible, though, is to postpone making a decision until you know the relevant facts. Most of this chapter is about how you do just that.

It is time for a concrete example. Suppose you have to decide whether to let your house while you are abroad on business. As soon as the question is raised, you think it would be better not to. Reasons why it would be a bad idea spring to your mind—the tenants might break things, they would certainly make the house dirty, you might not be able to arrange for them to leave when you want them to.

All this may be true, but before making your mind up there are at least two other aspects you need the facts on. First, is it in fact feasible to let your house for the period of time you have in mind? Secondly how much difference would letting the house make financially? You had considered only the practical aspects, no doubt dominated by an emotional reaction to the idea of someone else living in your home. That reaction might still be the deciding factor, but if you find out the facts first then you will have chosen to stick with your gut reaction rather than being simply controlled by it.

There is a vital difference between putting yourself in a position where you have to rationalize your decisions, because they were made on the basis of a prejudice you would feel foolish to acknowledge, and consciously deciding to discount the objectively preferable choice for personal and emotional reasons. That is why it is always worth taking time to collect information, even if in the end you do not allow it to determine your choice. You will not have to pretend to yourself or anyone else that your decision was made for all the right reasons. You will also be able to find out, and acknowledge, the usefulness or otherwise of your gut reactions.

An example may help to show how important it is to collect information relevant to your decision even when you end up discarding the facts entirely.

Alan Carpenter had to decide whether to attempt a reconciliation with his wife. She had left him a year previously for another man. She had come back to him saying that it had all been a mistake, a nightmare, and that she would never leave him again if he would only give her a second chance.

Alan spent some time talking to a very good friend of his, a marriage guidance counsellor, about his dilemma. He also looked into the financial implications of an attempted reconciliation. He and his wife had just about agreed a reasonable settlement between them, which would allow him to keep their home. The settlement had only to be made legal and binding, and Alan would be assured of his home and of the ability to start his life again.

By the time Alan made his decision he knew there were some very good reasons for not attempting a reconciliation. It was likely that it would not work, and even if it did their marriage would always be shaky. His friend had told him both the relevant statistics and the extent to which Alan's wife's infidelity would undermine their efforts to be equal partners in the marriage. Alan also knew he could easily lose his home second time round. His wife might well not feel so guilty if the marriage broke down again, and might become mean over financial matters. In any event, there would probably be a lengthy argument, leading to heavy solicitors' bills and a further delay before Alan could begin to build a new life.

Alan also knew that he was starting to recover emotionally from his wife's desertion. A second split could mean more emotional hell.

Knowing all this, Alan still decided to try again with his wife. Six months later, she left him again. Nothing could have made the second split painless. But Alan felt at least that he had gone back into the marriage with open eyes, that he had decided in spite of all the arguments to the contrary that he needed to give his marriage one more try. He did not consider himself to be a victim or a fool, but someone who had taken a risk to find out something important. His recovery from the second split was, I think, speeded up as a result of this attitude.

A practical step towards keeping an open mind

On a practical level, it is pretty difficult to live in a mental vacuum while you are trying to make a decision. You probably need to *do* something to control your anxiety. One thing you can do, at a very early stage, in fact at what we can call the pre-decision stage, is to plan a time-scale. Chapter Eight looks at the question of time-scales in detail, but here I simply want to draw attention to the possibility of using a planned time-scale to contain your anxiety and postpone a decision until the right time.

In the last chapter we considered the power of decision frames. You can use time-scale frames as a means of coming to terms with a period of uncertainty.

Let me give a concrete example of this. You will recall Susie Jeffreys' decision, the first discussed in this book. She avoided deciding whether to leave her husband or not for over a year, and this avoidance drove her into a frenzied social life, uneasy relationships with those about her, and sickness and stress for herself.

Given that this decision was one of the most difficult and important of her life, and that it affected not only her future happiness but that of her child, no-one could have expected her to make it in a hurry. There is a critical difference, however, between choosing not to make a decision yet, and running away from a decision.

This may seem a rather subtle point, but it is fundamental. It has to do with whether we feel in control, or at the mercy of fate and other people. Consider Susie's reaction when anyone asked her whether she was going to stay with her husband or leave. She burst into tears. She felt trapped by the question, pushed into thinking about something she couldn't face but vaguely felt she ought to.

Suppose she had decided to change nothing for six months. She might have had good reason to delay any final decision for a time. She might have wanted to see her daughter firmly established at school before making momentous decisions.

If she had chosen a time-scale for her decision, she could have lived honestly and without fear in the interim. She would not have been running away from a dark shadow all the time but would have allocated a definite time and place for that shadow to be confronted. She would have been in control. When friends asked her what she was going to do, she could have replied that she was waiting until September, the New Year, or whenever she had chosen. She could have told them why she had chosen that time-scale.

There is a world of difference between knowing you ought to go to the dentist sometime and having an appointment on 23rd May. Using time-scale frames for important decisions exploits this difference. If you feel you can't make a decision yet, you are probably right. But allot yourself a time when you will try to make it, and if you still can't make it then, allot yourself another time. To avoid indefinite procrastination keep a rough check on how often you have postponed any one decision. This will be part of the information contained in your 'Decision Diary' (see Chapter Ten).

Paradoxically, once you have chosen not to make an important decision for a set period of time, you may find that the relief frees you to make it immediately, but that is another story.

A second practical step towards keeping an open mind

When I was advising parents on how to help their children with reading difficulties, usually the most necessary advice was 'Don't worry about it'. Often the parents' anxiety was the root cause of the child's failure.

Yet to say 'Whatever you do, don't worry' had the effect of increasing the parents' anxiety, as they worried that their worry was affecting their child, and desperately tried not to ask questions, not to buy books, nor to visit the teacher, and not to test their child's progress.

When people are anxious, they need something positive to do. I used to give these parents all kinds of tasks, ranging from making lists of all the books they read aloud to their children, to making sure they watched one television programme each day with their child, to reading aloud a prescribed set of stories at bedtime. In fact it often didn't much matter what these tasks were, as long as they seemed sensible to the parents and did not centre round the child's reading performance.

So here is a second practical step for the anxious decision-maker, an activity with which you can busy yourself and which happens to be useful as well.

Instead of just trying *not* to decide, why not write a list of all the possible ways your decision could go? In other words, make lots of alternative decisions at this stage, rather than one prejudgement. Try this tactic, which we can call 'decision outcome brainstorming', on your next decision. Brainstorming is a technique commonly used in business to stimulate ideas and creative thinking. A theme is decided upon, and those present call out and jot down everything that comes into their heads on that theme. At the brainstorming stage nothing is rejected as foolish or inappropriate, the objective being to provoke as much spontaneity as possible. Here is an example of one of my 'decision outcome brainstorms':

Decision to be made: When shall I move from the country to the town?

Possible outcomes: — as soon as possible
— when my son starts school
— when my son starts secondary school
— when I change jobs
— when I can't afford to live here any longer
— when my son starts complaining about living 'miles from anywhere'
— when I see a house in town I like
— never
— not yet

Collecting information: the first step

Of course, collecting information is in itself an activity which can keep you busy and help you not to make your decision in too much haste. The sooner you start actively collecting, the sooner you are out of the danger zone of rushed decisions and into the safety of method and organization.

Having staved off that immediate urge to get your decision over with, you can now begin to assemble the evidence. First and foremost, you need a method which ensures that you investigate all the kinds of information which may be relevant. One of the most common mistakes people make when they are collecting information to reach a decision is to concentrate on one aspect of the evidence only. You might, for example, choose to move to a cheaper house because it will save you money and compare only the house prices while neglecting to consider removal costs, extra travelling to work and school, costs of making the new house into your own home, and so on.

So as a first step you need to examine the decision to be made and identify the different kinds of information you need. Write them down.

For example, suppose you are deciding on your holiday for this year. You want to choose the kind of holiday you should go on. Should it be to a hotel, an apartment, friends, camping, caravanning, or other? You will need information of the following kinds, at least:

Financial, such as how much each sort of holiday will cost
Practical, such as what the precise living arrangements would be in each case
Feasibility, of finding a holiday of each type in your preferred location
And of course, *personal*, how attracted are you by each sort of holiday?

Usually it is not difficult to find things out. What is more difficult is ensuring you have not 'forgotten' some important aspect, often because you were afraid of the implications of that particular item of information. A friend of mine chose to go and live with her husband in a house owned by him and his family. She assumed her rights to live in that house would be protected in the event of a marriage breakdown. She did not want to find out for certain if they would be; had she found out that such an arrangement would make her position in the home very vulnerable, that would have indicated that her husband and his family were prepared for her to be vulnerable in that way. She certainly did not want to face the implications of that attitude on the eve of her wedding.

This example shows again why collecting information is the worst bit of decision-making. You never know what you might find out. Yet if you rush this stage or carry it out in a biased or blinkered way, you have already compromised your decision-making before you really start.

Whenever you find out something relevant to your decisions, write it down. This prevents 'selective forgetting', where uncomfortable facts are conveniently forgotten and you remember only what you find acceptable. This totally destroys the point of collecting information in the first place.

Making notes

I cannot think of any substitute for writing when it comes to making sure none of the information you have collected is forgotten. Selective forgetting is so pernicious and its effects on decision-making so disastrous that making notes is essential, even though it is time-consuming and not necessarily something which comes naturally.

A cautionary tale seems appropriate at this point. Simon was trying to decide whether to go into business with a friend of his. One evening in the pub he had a brief but important conversation with someone whose opinion he respected. He did little more than quiz him on the trustworthiness of his friend. Simon realized that evening that he did not consider his friend to be trustworthy in general but had always assumed their friendship was such that he would be trustworthy towards him personally. He also realized that he knew in his heart of hearts that if and when things became difficult, he would not be able to rely on his friend.

Three months later Simon went into business with this friend. A year later the business folded and the friend ran off with any money he could lay his hands on. Simon lost, personally, about ten thousand pounds.

Not until then did he remember the conversation in the pub, and curse himself for having allowed it to slip from his mind. Of course, he had not wanted to remember it—he had been rather looking forward to setting up in business, and he had conveniently forgotten it.

Making notes on the information you collect is no guarantee against this kind of perceptual and memory bias, but it can help. You need to find a way of making notes which causes you least trouble and inconvenience. Perhaps you will have a decision notebook in which you jot things down at the end of the day. Perhaps you will have a box in which you collect all the scraps of paper you have recorded things down on. How you do it is up to you; whether you do it is likely to be fundamental to the success of your decision-making.

Don't be a slave to information

It isn't always necessary to collect a lot of information before making a decision. I think that the more important a decision is, the more necessary it is to ensure it isn't going to spring any nasty surprises on you. But it is better to discriminate between important and trivial decisions than slavishly to collect masses of information every time.

A schoolfriend of mine knew that she wanted to apply to Oxford University. Because of the collegiate structure of that particular university, she had to choose a college from about eight which took women at the time. She knew that this decision was trivial, in comparison with getting into Oxford in the first place. So she chose the college with the most beautiful gardens, and then got on with revising for her exams. She was successful, and never regretted her choice. Had she spent hours or days researching into the pros and cons of each college, she might have failed her exams.

Making a decision quickly on grounds which you know to be arbitrary because you have judged that decision to be trivial is different from refusing to consider the evidence on an important decision because you are overwhelmingly prejudiced towards one outcome.

Time to spend collecting information

How much time should you spend collecting information? The answer is, as much as you can. Not only will you collect more the longer you spend doing it, but your changing moods will enable you to collect different kinds of information at different times. What seemed to be the critical fact when you were excited two days ago now seems a minor point in the light of your current pessimism.

It is worth pausing to consider here whether people customarily save time by skimping on the information-gathering stage. I think that in fact the reverse is true. What commonly happens, particularly with difficult decisions, is that we spend a great deal of time thinking about the decision in a half-hearted way, generally fretting about it but not actually getting down to any solid information-gathering. We are in a truly vicious circle, too anxious to face the questions which need to be faced, with all those unanswered questions feeding our anxiety and undermining our will-power. If we do settle down and find out some facts and figures, this activity both concentrates our minds and relieves our anxiety. We become more relaxed and efficient, and time is saved.

4

Taking Advice Without Being Taken Over: Other People and Your Decisions

The right time to take advice

This chapter is concerned with how and when you can involve other people in your decision-making. It is concerned with consulting people on an informal basis, such as family and friends. The next chapter is concerned with taking professional advice. These chapters follow the chapter on collecting inform-ation because it is better to consult other people after you have begun to gather information for yourself. This is for two main reasons.

The first is that the early stages of information-gathering serve two purposes. One is, clearly, to provide you with some of the facts; the second is to clarify your thinking about the decision itself. During early information-gathering, you begin to under-stand exactly what your decision is likely to involve, and the time-scale within which it must be made. You 'frame' your decision appropriately, as we discussed in Chapter Two, and you therefore begin to ask the right questions in the right way. You become, to some extent, an expert on the decision which must be made. This puts you in a much better position to seek advice from other people.

The second reason for consulting others after you have spent some time collecting not only information but also your thoughts, is that you will be much less easily swayed by other people's opinions. Information and advice from those you consult will take their place with the other facts, ideas, gut feelings and prejudices which you have already accumulated. You will be able to discuss the issues with those you consult. You will never be asking them to tell you what to do; but you will be able to 'take advice'.

Suppose you have to decide which of two local secondary schools your daughter should attend. For the sake of this argument, I assume that you consider that this decision is your ultimate responsibility, not your daughter's, although her preference will be an important factor. If you ask family, friends and teachers for their advice too early, you are likely to hear, and possibly be swayed by, opinions based on ignorance, politics and vested interests. A fellow parent will advise you to send your daughter to the school his son attends. He wants tacit support for his own decision. The primary school headteacher's advice for your child may be coloured by a recent argument with one of the secondary school heads which has made her resolve to promote the other school.

If you have gathered some information for yourself on the locality, history, intake and staff of the two schools before you discuss the decision you have to make with these people, not only will you be better able to tell fact from opinion, but you will know which questions to ask to obtain the best advice from each party. You can ask your fellow-parent about transport and homework, the headteacher about the syllabus and sixth-form opportunities.

The right way to take advice

Some people refuse to take other people's advice on personal decisions. They may do so out of arrogance, secretiveness, pride or fear. Chapter Six deals with those decisions which you have to make alone. Most personal decisions, however, do not fall into that category. If you choose to make them alone, you lose the wealth of information and experience to be found in the people around you. You lose one of the resources uniquely available to us as human beings, the knowledge of our fellow human beings.

If on the other hand you come to depend too much on others, there are equal dangers. Not only will many of the decisions other people make for you affect your life adversely, since they will be based on feelings and prejudices quite inappropriate to you. More seriously, you will never have the opportunity to learn from your own good and bad decisions, and thus improve as a decision-maker and acquire increasingly more control over the course your life takes. So the key is to consult other people without losing control.

How not to use advice

Of course, if someone offers you advice and you decide not to take it, you need to be careful not to offend or annoy them. Hopefully most people will understand that you need to make your own decisions, and the best course of action is often just to point that out in a straightforward and friendly way. If you are consulting someone you know from past experience to be rather prickly and inclined to take offence, you can mention to him that further information has come to light which changes the picture somewhat, so allowing him to accept that his advice was of limited value without detracting from his self-esteem.

You can also almost always identify something in what he has said which has helped you, and focus on that rather than on what you decided not to use. I often say to people 'What you said about such-and-such really set me thinking, and I suddenly realized. . . .' In other words your friend's advice has been a useful input but not the determining factor. All but the most unreasonable of people will accept this role, and indeed be relieved that they do not carry the burden of determining your decision.

Sorting out what you want to ask

We have already discussed the importance of not consulting other people too early. If, like me, you are the kind of person who tends to rush off and talk to a friend almost before you know what you have to decide about, then you must practise waiting. You can use the time to plan who you are going to consult and what you are going to ask them. That way you will be in charge of the advice you eventually receive.

It can be helpful to write a list of those you intend to consult. Then, before you actually talk to them, write down for each one why they are a useful person to talk to. The questions you want to ask them will often follow from this. Here is an example list for deciding whether to buy a new car.

Who?	Why?
Dad	He knows a lot about cars
B and T Motors	They know current market values
Jeff	He services my current car

33

It is immediately clear from this that 'Dad' will be able to advise you on the range of cars you might buy, while 'B and T Motors' can tell you how much you will get for your old car and how much you will have to pay for different new cars. 'Jeff' can give you an estimate of how much your old car is likely to cost you in repairs and maintenance over the next few months.

Now think of a decision you must make in the near future. List the people you would consult, and why. As you are doing this, the questions you want to ask each of them are probably already coming to mind.

Two kinds of knowledge

You will certainly find it useful to consult people with two rather different kinds of knowledge. The first, more obvious, kind is knowledge about the area in which the decision is being made. In the example above, 'Dad' was consulted because he knew about cars, and the decision was about cars.

The other kind of knowledge, which is just as important, is knowledge about you, the decision-maker. It is often useful to consult someone who knows you very well. He can help you own up to some of your hidden motives for choosing one course of action rather than another. He can also predict some of the consequences of your decision which are likely to be particularly difficult or useful for you.

A close friend of mine was trying to decide whether to go into a shared house or rent a small flat on his own. He decided eventually on the flat. I pointed out to him that since he had to study in the evenings and since he was by nature a very sociable person, he would find it much easier to be living by himself rather than with friends.

The particular dangers in consulting friends

It is particularly tempting to hand over the responsibility for the decision itself to people you are close to. Not only is this a bad idea because, as we have said many times, you will lose control of your own life if you do this, but it can also result in your losing friends. If you have allowed a good friend to make your decision for you, you will be tempted to blame him if things go wrong.

34

There is a fine balance between taking advice from friends and taking instructions. It is up to you, the decision-maker, to find it.

There is a particular pattern which many spouses follow, usually with disastrous consequences. A joint decision of some importance has to be made, such as whether to have a child or whether to move house. One spouse, let's say the wife, for the sake of argument, avoids expressing a firm opinion. She is happy to listen to her husband talk about the decision, even discuss it with him in a rather noncommittal way, but she never makes a clear statement about what she personally would prefer to do. Often she may actually say 'I don't really mind either way, you decide', or perhaps her husband just eventually goes ahead, rightly convinced his wife will never come off the fence.

As one decision succeeds another in this fashion, their life becomes more and more determined by him alone rather than jointly. She appears content, but she will probably leave him. Even if she never actually walks out of the door she will leave him emotionally and mentally. By never actively participating in the decision-making she has reserved the right to opt out of the consequences. Her apparent acquiescence concealed a fundamental lack of commitment.

This pattern as I have described it is only relevant to people who are intending to build a joint life, and we look at how to take truly joint decisions later, in Chapter Eight. But the pattern can occur to a more limited extent between friends, and it illustrates one of the particular risks in consulting friends about decisions. Suppose a group of friends are planning a holiday together. Watch out for the one who seems content with whatever the others decide. He is most likely to drop out at the last minute, or be a bore on the holiday itself.

Consider carefully before you discuss an important decision with a close friend. Are you sure that you're not hoping they will take part or all of the responsibility away from you? That is a bad reason for asking their advice.

Cats and dogs

It is becoming clear that consulting family and friends is

35

primarily a question of walking a tightrope between two extremes. At one extreme you might take advice too soon, allow it to determine your decision rather than guide it, and rely too much on those around you. At the other extreme you might avoid consulting other people altogether and make all the important decisions in your life in isolation.

The first step to striking the right balance is to recognize which of the two extremes you personally are closer to. We can call these extremes the 'dog' decision-maker and the 'cat' decision-maker. The dog is too dependent on others and never really differentiates between those actions he is responsible for and those which are someone else's responsibility. The cat, as you would expect, is rather aloof and disengaged. You will be, by nature and habit, inclined towards 'dogginess' or 'cattiness'.

To help you decide which you are, and which your friends are, here are two lists, one of classic doggy characteristics and one of classic catty ones. Once you have decided which extreme you are closer to, we shall look at how dogs can become more catty, and vice versa. For clarity's sake, we shall look at extremes of dog and cat behaviour, although it is unlikely that you will find your own behaviour at either extreme.

Guidelines for dogs

Clearly the doggy decision-maker needs to become more catty, and vice versa. We shall begin by considering how the typical dog can become more discriminating in his advice-taking, and how he can remain in charge of his own decision-making throughout.

The dog needs to be particularly careful that he doesn't take advice too early. He will be tempted to take advice as a substitute for hard thinking of his own. He will almost certainly need to carry out the exercise described at the start of this chapter, where people to be consulted are listed together with the questions each can answer. He should ration himself, once he has started consulting people, to asking say, not more than one person's advice a day, and he should give himself a maximum number of people to consult about any one decision. If he is the kind of dog with an 'owner', one person whose

Dogs	Cats
Everyone knows what's going on in the dog's life.	The cat is rather secretive, and people say they 'don't *really* know him'.
As soon as a tricky decision comes up, the dog tells someone about it.	The cat ponders a decision alone for a long time and even then may consult no one.
If the decision goes wrong, the dog may well say 'Why didn't you tell me that would happen?'	If the decision goes wrong, the cat licks his wounds in private.
You wish the dog would show a bit more maturity.	You wish the cat would open up.
If the decision turns out to be a good one, the dog throws a party.	If the decision turns out to be a good one, the cat treats himself to something nice.
When the dog consults you, you feel bored.	When the cat consults you, you feel honoured.
The dog either canvasses a lot of different opinions, or has one 'owner' who he is constantly turning to.	The cat never discusses his decision in a crowd, and he rarely asks the same person for advice more than once.

advice he asks about almost everything, then sooner or later he must choose a decision to make without involving his 'owner' at all.

When he has decided on a course of action, he should write down what he has decided to do. This will help him to 'own' the decision himself, to acknowledge that ultimately it is his responsibility.

For the dog trying to break his doggy habits, any form of

37

activity is better than talking about the decision. He can write about the decision, as long as he doesn't write *to* anyone; he can dig the garden whenever he feels the urge to telephone his 'owner'; he can talk to people about something completely different. This last course of action is risky, however. It is surprising how the conversation can work its way round to the decision in hand, especially if the dog's friends are used to hearing about his problems.

These guidelines may seem rigid and artificial. In the early stages of breaking doggy habits, I think this level of rigidity is necessary. You are not only attempting to break ingrained habits of your own, but you are trying to establish a new pattern of relating to your family and friends.

Guidelines for cats

In some ways, cats have an easier task. They do not have to stop doing something; they have to start doing something. Cats need to start involving other people in their decision-making.

One way of doing this is for them to become more free with their own advice. Cats are frequently generally reticent, believing that just as they prefer to run their lives alone so other people will not welcome advice from them. The pattern can be broken by the cat making helpful suggestions when the opportunity arises. Cats are very commonly good listeners, unlike dogs, and so they are well placed to find an opportunity to give a helpful opinion or relevant example from their own experience. Once the cat has demonstrated in this way that a change is in order, his family and friends will be more likely to show an increased interest in his affairs if he begins to discuss them.

For the cat who values his privacy highly, there is the time-honoured stratagem of asking advice on behalf of an imaginary friend/cousin/acquaintance. What is often not fully appreciated is that it doesn't matter if your listener sees through the 'I've got a friend with a problem' opener. The essential thing is that the cat doesn't have to admit that the affairs under discussion are in fact his affairs. Even if the truth is suspected, it is not known, and the cat's private life is not infringed to the extent it would be if he openly identified himself.

We must also consider the case of the paranoid cat. This individual fears that whatever he reveals may be used against him. He may simply fear ridicule, or that others will actually spoil his plans if they know what those plans are. Paradoxically, the best approach for the paranoid cat is to tell all the details to everyone. Then the matter ceases to be a secret at all, it loses its emotional potency, both for the paranoid cat and for his listener, and of course the rest of the world is much less likely to gossip about it or use it if it is completely in the open.

Unfortunately, the paranoid cat often 'tests the water' by divulging a few details to one or two people. This approach is likely to end up in his worst fears being realized. He will feel extremely vulnerable with a precious secret entrusted to just a couple of others, and they will be so excited by the atmosphere of secrecy that they will find it difficult to be calm and considerate.

One of the problems for the paranoid cat is that he vividly imagines harm that could be done to him by people whose advice he might seek but he does not see the harm he may do himself by living in isolation from the opinion of others. It may help him actually to work out quite concretely the worst that could happen as a result of his consulting, say, a particular friend. It may be that when he confronts his fear and suspicion in that way they become less powerful and he is freed to be a little more open.

Case history of a paranoid cat. Helen worked for a large manufacturing company. She had started as a programmer five years previously but had been wanting to move into general management for a couple of years. A job as a junior manager in the company fell vacant and several existing members of staff applied. Helen wasn't sure whether to or not.

She did not know whether she would be at a significant disadvantage because she had been in programming for quite a long time and had never run a team. She was not sure what experience the other applicants had, nor precisely what was being looked for.

There were a lot of people within the company who could have given her useful information but she did not want people to know she was looking for a change. She felt she would be embarrassed if she didn't succeed and people had known she was keen. She also felt it might prejudice her chances of promotion within the programming department. These were good reasons for not discussing the matter with people at work. In addition, Helen was by nature a reserved, if not secretive, person, always anxious not to give anything away, a typical paranoid cat.

In the end, Helen decided not to apply for the job. She had to make that decision on very limited information, which she felt wasn't adequate. It is also interesting that she did not discuss things with anyone outside work either, because she was worried word might get back to the office and also because she didn't want to give the impression of being vacillating, discontented or over-ambitious. Again, she feared that to give such an impression would be damaging to her, so she passed up the chance of getting the job she wanted.

Information and advice

In this chapter I have not drawn a distinction between asking people for information and asking them for advice or their opinion. In theory, information is fact, and advice and opinion are a mixture of fact and interpretation. In practice I think that people always give a mixture of the two.

This means that whenever someone tells you something of relevance to your decision you have to consider not only what you have been told but also who told you. Sometimes it is easy. When a recently divorced friend advises you against marriage, for example, you are likely to take her advice with a pinch of salt. Sometimes, however, it is easy to fall into the trap of regarding someone else's 'facts' as truly objective.

There are a few situations in which it is particularly easy to make this mistake.

The expert adviser. When you ask someone for information who can reasonably be assumed to be knowledgeable in that area, it is tempting to treat what he tells you as fact. If you have a friend who is a primary school teacher and you are deciding which school to send your child to, you may consider the information she gives you on different approaches to teaching reading to be reliable and true. Knowledge in a subject area is no safeguard against prejudice, however. Even experts have axes to grind. You can afford to be no less vigilant when you ask an expert for information than when you ask a non-expert. Perhaps your teacher friend is biased in favour of the method used in her own school. She will describe it more attractively than she will other methods. Perhaps she is keen to impress you. She will describe experimental methods as if they were well understood. Perhaps she has a child of her own with reading difficulties. That will influence profoundly anything she says about teaching reading.

The reassuring adviser. If someone tells you what you have been hoping to hear, you will be irresistibly tempted to believe them. This situation is particularly likely to occur when you have half-made your decision. In a similar way, people who tell you things which appear to simplify your decision, make your choice clear-cut and straightforward, are likely to be viewed as particularly reliable sources of information.

The likeable adviser. People we like are much more convincing and easy to believe than people we dislike. Also, if we want to be liked by someone, we don't question what they say. If we don't care about them, we either take what they say on its merits or disagree with it on principle. It is possible to become part of a vicious circle, where we choose people to be our friends because we like what they say and we believe what they say because they are our friends. This is cosy and comfortable, but not conducive to that kind of decision-making which brings about constructive change.

How to tell fact from fiction. The implication of this section on information and advice is that we have to remember that all information we are given may be coloured by the particular views and belief system of the giver. We have to be especially vigilant when the information we are given is expert, reassuring or from a likeable source.

How can we tell when information is biased, and how can we

make sure we remember to check? Here are five questions to ask yourself when someone gives you an important piece of information bearing on a decision you are making.

- Has the information-giver anything to gain if I decide one way or the other?
- Has the information-giver anything to lose if I decide one way or the other? (Things to gain and lose include money, status, influence, face.)
- Does the information-giver have strong political, religious or other views which might influence him in this area?
- Has the information-giver had any personal experience which might have biased his view?
- Is the information-giver under the influence of anyone with something to gain or lose from my decision?

It is very unlikely that the answer to all these questions will be no. But once you have asked them, you will be better placed to allow for the bias in the information you receive. You can balance the people whose advice you seek so that the bias cancels itself out. Or you can simply adjust the amount of salt you take with the information.

Bad reasons for consulting other people

It is clear from this chapter that I consider consulting other people to be an important part of most effective decision-making. While recognizing it to be an activity fraught with the twin dangers of being misled and being taken over, it is vital in providing the decision-maker with information and comment to guide his thinking and provoke rethinking. So the right reason for consulting other people is because you want to find things out.

Often, however, we consult others for the wrong reasons. Then our decision-making is unlikely to be assisted at all by doing so. Here are seven common bad reasons for consulting other people, so that you can check that none of them is your reason next time.

- *You want them to agree with you*. Unless the person you consult cares about you very much, he will agree with you as soon as he sees that's what you really want and so you will have learned nothing.

- *You want someone to blame if things go wrong.* This is a very bad reason and as we have already discussed could lose you friends and a lot more besides.
- *You want them to like you.* As a start to a friendship asking advice isn't very auspicious, since it sets the relationship off on an asymmetric footing. And asking someone for advice when you desperately want them to like you means you are in no state to assess calmly the information they give you.
- *You want attention.* You should never undervalue yourself to the extent that you use important decisions in your life as conversation openers or bridges to social success.
- *You want a shoulder to cry on.* Crying on shoulders is often necessary, but don't confuse it with getting advice.
- *You want to influence them.* Pretending to ask someone something when really you want to tell them something is dishonest.
- *Other people think you ought to.* Try reading this book again from the beginning.

5

Expensive Decisions:
Taking Professional Advice

What is meant by 'professional' advice

Chapter Four was concerned with the care you must take when consulting other people informally about your decisions. This chapter is concerned with formal advice, and even more care is needed here.

I define professional advice as advice which costs you money. It is not to be confused with advice from a friend who happens to be an accountant, or a cousin who happens to be a solicitor. Professional advice is uniquely valuable precisely because it costs you money. You will take it more seriously because you paid for it and, indeed, the more you pay for it, the more seriously you are likely to take it. Your adviser has a clear commitment to provide good advice, since he can be sued for not doing so. Your rights are clearly defined, and so is his commitment.

I also include as professional advisers people whose services are not paid for by you personally but, in whole or in part, by the State on your behalf. These can be, for example, doctors, dentists, and marriage guidance counsellors. The discussion in this chapter applies to them just as it applies to those advisers who are costing you money personally. Their advice is not free, and your rights and responsibilities vis à vis that advice are the same.

Some advice is classed as professional because the person giving it is being paid for doing so, although particular consultations are not charged for as such. A typical example of this kind of role is a bank manager. The guidelines in this chapter apply to these people too.

When you need professional advice

Because it is expensive, professional advice must be taken sparingly and used well. It is necessary when one or both of two conditions prevail:

44

1. You need specialist information of the kind only a professional can give.
2. You need to consult someone within the kind of formal framework a professional situation provides.

Let me clarify the distinction between these two conditions. If you are deciding whether to divorce your husband, you may need precise information on your legal rights, the steps you can take, the position you will be in after you have taken them, and so on. Condition One prevails, and you need to pay for a solicitor's advice.

You may also, or alternatively, need an objective and professional view of your marriage, its future, and your own development within the marriage, of your reasons for thinking of ending it and your expectations of life alone. Condition Two prevails, and you need to pay for a family therapist's advice.

Under Condition One, you are paying for information. Under Condition Two, you are paying for objectivity and professional commitment. It is possible that you can save money under Condition One by buying relevant books and papers. You will certainly lose a lot of time, and you may also miss out on important 'inside' information which it is very difficult for a layman to obtain, such as the favourite judgements of different judges. It is possible that you can save money under Condition Two by using friends or acquaintances as counsellors. It is highly unlikely that they will be objective or committed. I think that for certain types of personal decision, professional advice is indispensable. How expensive it turns out to be is largely up to you.

The brick wall principle

The guiding principle which dictates both whether you need professional advice at all and, if you do, when precisely during the total decision-making process you need it, is one which I call the brick wall principle. If you feel you have reached a brick wall, which prevents your progressing your decision-making, then you may well be at a point when professional advice is the only thing which will move you on.

The brick wall principle assumes that you have already

engaged in all the other decision-making activities we have described so far, yet despite your accumulation of information, and consultation with any appropriate friends and acquaintances, you feel you are still some way from being able to make the decision. More than that, you do not know what to do next. You have done as much as you can by yourself. Now you need reliable and qualified input from an external source.

You have reached a brick wall because there is information you need which you cannot acquire on your own. You require professional advice under Condition One, described above, which will give you the information you need. You may alternatively have reached a brick wall because your own pattern of thinking and feeling about the particular decision you are trying to make is taking you round and round in circles. You require professional advice under Condition Two, which will break your pattern of thinking and feeling and help you to see the decision in a new light.

Preparing for the consultation

When you believe you have identified a requirement for professional advice, write down why you need to consult a professional and, if it is because Condition One prevails, what information you need from him precisely. Suppose you are deciding whether to declare some income for tax purposes or not. You probably need to consult an accountant. What information do you want from him? Your list of questions might look like this:

1. If I declare this income, how much tax will I be liable for?
2. Can I declare it in such a way that my tax liability is reduced or eliminated?
3. If I don't declare it, what are the likely consequences?
4. If I don't declare it, and the Inland Revenue find out, can I justify my not declaring it?

Making a list like this will ensure, under Condition One, that there really is information you cannot obtain without paying for it. It will also identify for you the information you have to provide your professional adviser with for him to do his job

46

properly. In the example above, you will have to provide him with details of all your other income for him to answer question 1, and also details of your personal circumstances. This approach enables you to make the best use of the accountant's expensive time.

How much advice?

Once you have a clear idea of what you need professional advice for, you can begin to work out how much advice you are likely to need. Almost always, you pay for professional advice by the hour. I have known therapists who charge according to their degree of success, but this is unusual, and of course there are agents who will charge commission rather than bill you for their time direct. But generally the more of a professional's time you take up, the more you have to pay. So that is one strong reason for minimizing the amount of advice you buy.

There is another less obvious but equally cogent argument for cutting down as much as possible the amount of a professional's time you take up. The more time you spend with a professional adviser, the less efficient use you will make of his time. If you know you have a limited time, you are more likely to plan your own use of that time carefully and stick to that plan. Also, and relatedly, the more time you spend with a professional adviser, the more he will be part of the scenery rather than an agent for change.

So select the points at which you need professional advice on the brick wall principle, and then take the minimum amount of professional time necessary to get over that brick wall. Initially, it is wise to book a single consultation. Use this consultation to make a judgement on the competence of the adviser you have selected. Then, if at all possible, use it to plan how many more consultations you will require.

Try to avoid an open-ended commitment. In particular, try to avoid any arrangement of the form 'We'll meet until the problem is solved/you have what you need/there's no further reason to meet'. Tell your adviser what you want to achieve, and ask him to give you an estimate of how long it will take to achieve it. Here are some examples of objectives to aim for with a professional adviser, to give an idea of the form they should take.

1. To find out what qualifications I need to become a chartered accountant.
2. To establish what would be involved in going into business in partnership with my brother.
3. To establish the cost of building an extension to my house.
4. To draw up my will.
5. To arrange care, custody and control of the children between my ex-husband and myself.
6. To stop feeling angry with my brother and his wife.

Whose advice?

It is fair to say that whatever kind of decision you need professional advice for, there is someone somewhere qualified to give it. Often it is easy to identify the kind of professional you want. For financial decisions, you need an accountant; for decisions with legal implications, a solicitor; for medical problems, a doctor; and so on.

Occasionally you know you need professional advice, but do not know what would be the appropriate profession. The Citizens' Advice Bureau may then be able to identify an appropriate professional for you, or friends may have had experience of looking for advice in that area.

Once you have identified the type of professional you need, you face the much more difficult task of selecting one in particular. If you have identified a clear requirement for professional advice and analysed carefully what you need it for, then buy the best advice you can afford. It may not always be the most expensive, but it is unlikely to be the cheapest.

Be careful, however, not to fall into the trap of thinking that just because someone's advice is expensive it must be good. Some advisers can charge highly because they are well-known and established. They may no longer be applying themselves energetically to solving problems. Others may be providing good advice to most people, but for a reason particular to your situation they give you poor advice. An expensive accountant used to dealing with large companies may be poorly informed and badly motivated when asked to consider the tax problems of a small company with a low turnover.

When you think of the money you spend on things which are of trivial significance in your life, it puts into perspective the amounts of money you spend on good quality advice, which can affect fundamental decisions. The extra insight that a single professional consultation can provide into an important decision is often critical to the quality of that decision.

Make a list of all the people whose advice you have paid for. For each one, mark whether you now consider it to have been money well spent. If you have wasted good money on professional advice, perhaps it was because you did not prepare for it in the way I suggested above. But it may have been because the advice you were given was poor. As we have discussed, paying money does not guarantee its value.

Finding the best adviser

There are several steps you can take which, whilst not guaranteeing that you will find the best adviser, will ensure that the adviser you choose is at least competent.

1. If there is a relevant society, trade association, or other licensing body for the kind of professional you are seeking to employ, consider only people who are on their list. Not only does this usually ensure a minimum level of competence, but it also often provides a means for obtaining redress if things go wrong.

2. If any of your friends, family or acquaintance have used professional advice of the kind you need, or know about professional advisers in the relevant area, ask them to recommend one, or better, a few. Personal recommendation by someone you know and trust is by far the best guide. I chose my accountant, my solicitor and the architect who designed my house on that basis. In any case, ask your family and friends about their experiences, and use them to become more knowledgeable about what you can realistically expect from professionals of that kind.

3. Once you have made a preliminary choice, try to contact one or two people who have used this person. Professionals should not mind your asking them to provide the names of a

couple of previous clients as references. If they cannot or will not do so, that is in itself a danger sign. Of course, professionals such as solicitors and doctors cannot disclose the names of their clients. Then you will have to rely on your own detective work.

4. Try to find out what kind of work the person or people you have chosen specialize in professionally . They will tend to do that best, and also more quickly and hence more cheaply.

5. Some professionals, such as some accountants and solicitors, will let a new client 'sample' a small amount of their advice free. If you have the opportunity and time to take advantage of this, 'sample' two or three possibles and compare them. Take a limited aspect of your decision to each, the same aspect to each for purposes of comparison, and discover what kind of advice each offers. Things to watch out for are:

- How comfortable do you feel talking to this person? It is no good employing someone to advise you if their very presence gives you extra problems. You should feel confident in his ability but not intimidated, relaxed but not careless. You should find him pleasant and reasonably likeable, but not so attractive that that is likely to become more important than the quality of his advice.

- How quickly and how thoroughly does he grasp what you are saying? It will save you time and money if you and he are on similar wavelengths, and if he is a good listener.

- How easy do you find it to understand him? Without prompting, he should use concepts and terminology which are comprehensible to you. The vast majority of useful advice can be given in the language of the reasonably intelligent layman.

Never forget that all these people want your custom. Just as much as someone who is selling you a car or a house, they are the ones who should convince you they have something worth selling.

Handling the consultations

The key thing to remember when taking professional advice is that you are in charge. It is very tempting to sink into, for example, the solicitor's comfortable chair and let him make the decisions, but you cannot afford to, literally or metaphorically. For every hour you spend with your professional adviser, you should spend several hours of your own time, preparing for the consultation, considering the implications of the advice he has given you, working out what to do next. His time is expensive, yours is free. Not only that, you are the one who has the complete picture and the motivation really to apply yourself to making a good decision. However good your adviser is, you are to him at the end of the day just another client. If you go to the consultations with a positive and responsible frame of mind, you are already most of the way towards ensuring you make the best use of them.

Here are some further practical ways of handling the consultations:

1. Make out an agenda. You will probably not write this agenda down formally, but it is up to you to make sure both you and your adviser know what the meeting or telephone call is for and can recognize when the objectives have been met.
2. Take notes. Not only is this important for all the obvious reasons, but it preserves the right balance between you and your adviser. It demonstrates that you are taking the consultation seriously. Nothing is worse than being left simply waiting while your adviser makes his own notes or answers an incoming telephone call. (Make sure, by the way, that you are not charged for any time he spends answering the phone while you are there.)
3. Use every minute constructively. Don't spend time in social chat, other than what is necessary to preserve a reasonably friendly atmosphere. You should be as charming as you can, since even professional advisers work better for people they like, but you should be charming in a time-efficient way. Witty asides are infinitely preferable to lengthy anecdotes.

4. Without being aggressive or unpleasant, take any opportunity you can to make it clear that it is you who are paying for the consultation. You may say, for example, 'I wonder if it would be better if I wrote the first draft of this letter since it might be rather expensive if you do the whole thing.' Never give the impression that money is no object, or your adviser will find it hard to resist the temptation to spend yours freely. Discuss terms of payment calmly and openly. Leave nothing to do with the financial contract between you ambiguous.

5. Take any opportunity you can to thank your adviser explicitly for a particularly useful piece of information or insight. Everyone works better when they are appreciated. Also, providing you thank your adviser in a thoughtful appraising way rather than in a patronizing or ingratiating way you will again be giving him the fundamental message that you are in charge.

6. At the moment you realize you have lost your grasp of what he is saying to you, ask him to explain. Often we are in some distress or agitation when we are taking professional advice. It can be easy to let our thoughts wander, and fail to follow a line of reasoning or explanation which our adviser is pursuing. It is vital then that we ask him to repeat what he has said, so that we are never agreeing to things we did not fully understand, or fumbling along, hoping everything will come clear eventually. To use our advisers effectively, we must keep abreast of them.

7. Be firm with yourself about sticking to questions the professional can uniquely answer when you are with him. You cannot expect your accountant to tell you how much it will prey on your mind if you don't declare some of your income. So don't waste time, and therefore money, discussing that with him.

Some consultation patterns to avoid

There are some unhelpful patterns it is easy to slip into when taking advice from an expert. The patterns I shall describe have in common that they reduce the amount of information you obtain from your adviser and in addition militate against your making the best use of the information you do obtain. These patterns exert their harmful effects by unbalancing the relationship between you and your professional adviser and by emphasizing his skill to the detriment of your own.

Pattern One: The Genius and the Fool. Advisers encourage this pattern by indulging in unnecessarily complex arguments and explanation, by using long words in preference to short ones, and by drawing attention to their qualifications. A particular danger sign is any insistence on their part on being addressed by a title such as Doctor or Professor. As seekers of advice, we encourage this pattern by beginning a consultation with 'Of course I don't know anything about this', by looking puzzled but never asking any questions, and by having nothing to say at the end of the consultation.

Pattern Two: Mother and Child. Advisers encourage this pattern by calling you 'dear', by making you a cup of tea, and by conveying to you in words and gestures that everything will turn out all right in the end. Advisers like this are particularly pernicious because they can feel so reassuring. However, by encouraging you to rely on them completely they are actually behaving very dangerously. We encourage the pattern when we become over-emotional during consultations, when we tell the adviser a lot of irrelevant detail about our personal lives, and when we arrange frequent consultations at regular intervals.

Pattern Three: The Knight and the Damsel. As is immediately obvious, this pattern only applies when a woman is seeking advice from a man. Male advisers encourage it by becoming angry on behalf of their client, by being over-solicitous about their client's health, finances and situation, and by asking their client out to dinner. Women clients encourage it by overdressing for consultations, by behaving in an inappropriately feminine manner (this is not to be confused with using a bit of female charm), and by accepting advice passively. Adviser/client relationships based on this pattern may lead to many things but are unlikely to assist the client in effective decision-making.

Pattern Four: The Rock and the Drowning Man. We discussed in Chapter Three how difficult it is to live with the uncertainty which surrounds an important decision. In situations of uncertainty and stress, it is tempting to try and identify something or somebody as utterly reliable and safe. A professional adviser can appear ideal material for a rock in stormy seas. Unfortunately, few advisers are utterly reliable and safe. We should never lose sight of the fact that we may need to change our adviser, or at least argue with him.

Even advisers qualified in various forms of therapy are not solid rocks, but people who bring their own flaws and rough edges to each consultation. And the people for whom this book is written are not drowning men, but people who are at turning points, where they need to exercise more, not less, control than usual. If you can hardly wait from one consultation to the next, if you suspend action between consultations, and if you never find anything to criticize in your adviser, then you have probably fallen into the 'Rock and the Drowning Man' trap.

If you take the steps that were outlined above on handling consultations then you should avoid all of these unhelpful patterns. If by any chance you find you have slipped into one, you may need to change your adviser. For not only are consultations based on an unhelpful pattern uninformative, they also positively undermine your effectiveness as a decision-maker.

6

Be Your Own Worst Enemy: Taking Decisions Alone

It is clear from the last two chapters that I consider that a lot can be gained from involving other people in your decision-making, if they are involved on the right terms. There are some decisions, however, which you may make entirely alone. Perhaps they are so personal you do not wish to discuss them with anyone. Perhaps they need to be kept an absolute secret. Perhaps you feel it is time to make a decision completely alone, to reinforce your own feelings of responsibility and control.

Reasons for taking decisions alone

There are good reasons and bad reasons for taking decisions alone. Some examples will help to clarify the difference.

A decision taken alone for a good reason: establishing independence

Jenny had recently made a major change in career direction. She had been teaching and assessing disturbed children, but with the birth of her first child and the break-up of her marriage soon afterwards, she felt she needed a complete change. She wanted to work with adults rather than children, since much of her emotional energy was now needed for her own daughter. For a long time she had wanted to study medicine, and she applied for a place at the medical school in her home town. She was accepted, and began the course in the September following her application. Her daughter was two by then.

Within a few weeks, it became clear to Jenny that studying medicine was even more demanding than she had thought it would be. In the past, she had always been a conscientious student, preferring to do more work than was expected rather than less. Now she found she had to miss lectures and rush through assignments without fully mastering their content. This preyed on her mind. She found she could not relax: either her daughter needed her or she felt she should be studying. Not only this, but she saw little prospect of the relentless pressure ending. She began to appreciate the extent to which it was assumed that a doctor's first commitment was to his work, not to his family. She saw years stretching ahead in which her daughter would have to take second place to her career.

She did not want that for her daughter. She did not want it for herself. Subtly, she became aware that she was studying medicine largely in order to put meaning and purpose into her life. She faced the fact that she should be looking for that meaning in herself and in her relationship with her daughter, not in the relentless pressure of external demands.

Jenny knew by Christmas that she was reaching a crisis point. She could not continue with medicine unless she was firmly committed to it. She had to decide once and for all whether she could, and should, make that commitment.

Jenny made that decision on her own. She decided, in fact, to give up medicine, and pursue a less impressive but still interesting career in industry, one which would enable her to put her daughter first in the evenings and at weekends, one which did not hold out any false promises of giving meaning to her life.

There are two main reasons why Jenny took that decision alone. The first was that she had recently relied a great deal on other people's advice. This decision was just the latest in a whole series of difficult choices she had had to make. Because of her temperament and the suddenness with which some of the decisions had been forced upon her, she had depended heavily on a particular group of close friends. These friends had talked things over with her until the early hours, had let her ring them up late at night, had been a constant source of good sense and support. Jenny felt that she owed it to them and to herself to show that she was now beginning to stand on her own two feet again.

The second reason why Jenny took this decision alone was that she knew it would be very painful and could be a source of regret. She wanted to be absolutely sure she took full responsibility for it, that looking back she would never be able to blame anyone else or claim they had influenced her at a time of stress. She would have to live with the decision for the rest of her life and she had to be extra careful that she was making up her own mind.

Obviously Jenny discussed her decision with tutors, family and friends. But she had made up her mind before these discussions, and knew that nothing they could say would alter it.

A decision taken alone for a bad reason: seeing other people's views as irrelevant

Nick was about to take up a two year residential place in business studies at a university some eighty miles from where he currently lived. He owned his own house, and needed to decide whether to sell it or let it. He had enough money saved to cover his living costs over the next two years, so he did not have to sell his house. Renting it out would just about cover the mortgage repayments.

Nick didn't believe in asking other people's advice. He considered his affairs to be his own business, and his alone, and did not think other people could tell him anything useful. It never crossed his mind to discuss whether he should sell his house with any of his friends, family or colleagues. In this, he was following a well-established pattern. Within the previous few months alone he had decided to apply for the place in business studies, to sell his car, to resign from his job, all decisions made without consulting anyone else.

It was not that Nick found the decision whether to sell or rent his house easy. He recognized the numerous considerations, such as the possible nuisance value of still being responsible for a property measured against the value of the investment, the likelihood of being able to sell his house easily against the problem of where to store his possessions if he did so. It was simply that Nick could not conceive of its having anything to do with anyone else.

How to tell the good from the bad

The distinction between good and bad reasons for taking decisions alone is relevant to the effectiveness of those decisions. Good reasons mean the decision is likely to be effective, bad that it is likely to be ineffective. (Remember that an effective decision brings about desirable changes to your life, an ineffective one surprising and unpleasant changes.) Good reasons imply you will put extra effort into the decision, recognizing that it is likely to be more difficult to decide well and that you are the only one who can ensure you decide well. Bad reasons imply you are un-informed, arrogant, or frightened of advice, or some mixture of these three, and so the foundations of your decision-making are flawed. Good reasons imply you are varying your decision-making habits to suit the decision, bad that you are treading familiar paths unthinkingly.

Here is a set of questions to ask yourself if you are considering making a decision alone. You can also use them to check out a lone decision you have already made. The more of them you can answer with 'yes', the more likely you are to make an effective lone decision.

- Are you apprehensive about making this decision alone?
- Is this the first decision you have made alone?
- Is this the first decision you have made alone for a little while?
- Have you ever thought in terms of its being 'necessary' to take this decision alone?
- Can you think of various people you might have liked to talk to about this decision?

Obviously the main danger when you need to make a decision alone is that your decision-making will be biased, your information-gathering incomplete, and your real motives unrecognized.

To avoid these pitfalls as much as possible, you need to try yourself to be as many different people as you can. Here are ten ways to go about this.

1. *Think about the decision at different times of day.* It is well known that our moods change with the time of day. Some of us leap out of bed in the morning enthusiastically, and become more dispirited as the day progresses. Others of us are at our calmest and most rational in the middle of the day. Still others find we can only be creative in the

evenings. You can exploit this variability to shed new light on your decision-making. Write down as many pros and cons as you can one morning, as soon as you wake up. Write down some more one afternoon. Stay up late one night and think of yet more.

2. *On a day when the last thing you want to do is think about the decision force yourself to*. You will think of completely different aspects when you are depressed from those you think of when you are buoyant.

3. *Read as many books and articles as you can which are relevant to your decision*. Books and articles can take part of the place of human advisers. They may look at an issue from a different perspective which suddenly introduces new factors into your decision-making. A friend of mine who was trying to decide whether to have minor cosmetic surgery did not want to discuss it with any of her acquaintances. She wanted to be sure her decision was determined by what she wanted to look like and not by how others saw her or liked to see her. She considered that her physical appearance was too important for her to risk undue influence from those she knew. So she read both women's magazine articles and medical books and journals voraciously for about six months before finally making up her mind. It is always a good idea to read different kinds of literature, to go out of your way to include books or articles you would never bother with in the normal course of events. As I have said already, lone decision-makers need all the help they can get.

4. *Imagine you are different people*. Whether you can in fact do this or not depends on how easily you find you can imagine yourself in someone else's shoes. If you can, act out the part of a teacher, a doctor, your mother, your wife, a good friend. See what arguments you bring to bear on the decision when you are pretending to be these other people.

5. *Imagine you are sitting opposite your worst critic*. This can be extremely enlightening. It can be even more enlightening than actually sitting opposite him, since you will

imagine that he will spot all the weak points you are conscious of in your position and that he will attack them much more strenuously than he would be likely to in reality. If you can justify your decision to your imagined worst critic it is probably fairly sound. Of course, there is always the temptation to cheat, and make your worst critic rather feeble in his arguments. If you find yourself doing that, it is a warning sign of an important worry lurking somewhere.

6. *Write down all the possible outcomes*. Do this for all the choices you might make. Again, do it at different times of the day, in different moods, when you are drunk as well as sober.

7. *Force yourself not to think about your decision for a day or two*. As soon as your mind returns to it, think of something else or busy yourself with something absorbing. You might read a novel, dig the garden, play loud music, cook, ring up friends, whatever — anything to take your mind off the decision. Then at the end of the allotted time, re-read all you have written with a fresh eye.

8. *Think of the worst that could happen, and the best*. What would you like to come out of this decision, in your wildest dreams? What do you fear from it, in your blackest nightmares?

9. Speaking of dreams, *try to remember your dreams*. Interpret them for clues about your hidden wishes and fears. There are two quite separate schools of thought about dreams and their interpretation which suggest that they can be useful to the aspiring effective decision-maker. One is that the content of the dreams themselves contains your repressed wishes and fears, often in symbolic form. In this case, pondering your dreams will provide you with invaluable, if painful, information. Another school of thought says simply that when people interpret their own dreams they find it possible to say things they would not have dared to say 'cold'. It is as if the dream itself gives them permission to speak out. To give an example, let us suppose a woman dreams that she

goes into an empty house and falls down the stairs. This kind of dream is quite common. She interprets it by saying that she felt her husband never loved her (empty house) and that was the cause of various disasters in her life (falling downstairs). It may be that the dream truly did mean that. Or it may be that interpreting the dream gave her an opportunity to say something painful she could not have said otherwise. You can see how, even if the second view is correct, you can learn new things about important decisions by consciously interpreting dreams as relevant to those decisions.

It is also possible to view dreams as 'thoughts you have when you are asleep'. Just as you think rather differently about things when you first wake up from last thing at night, so you think even more differently when you are asleep. So the lone decision-maker should use the thoughts he has when he is asleep just as he uses thoughts from different times of day, in different moods, and so on.

10. *Make the decision, but don't act on it for a few days.* Examine how you feel. Is it as if a weight had been lifted from your shoulders? Or do you feel under sentence? Perhaps your decision is responsible for these feelings. Maybe you should review it.

A final point

It may be worth considering taking professional advice (see previous chapter) for a completely confidential objective view on a personal or secret matter. Even if you take the kind of precautions listed above, it will be difficult on your own to prevent unrecognized bias and repressed motives influencing a major personal decision. Perhaps you cannot obtain a different viewpoint from a friend or relation, however, because you don't want to involve anyone you know in this discussion. Professional advice may be the only option, as professional advisers are required to maintain strict confidence. This is a separate reason for seeking professional advice from those discussed in the previous chapter.

7

Enter the Jury:
Weighing Up the Pros and Cons

If you follow the suggestions in this book, you will come to a point in your decision-making where you have accumulated facts, opinions, advice and ideas, all relevant to the decision which must be made. How are you to take all these into account, whilst bearing in mind their differing degrees of importance?

The Systematic Approach

People find it very difficult to take a lot of different factors into account when making a single decision. Unwelcome facts are forgotten, unlikely but disastrous outcomes assume undue significance, and the bias you went to such pains to eliminate at the information-gathering stage now rears its persistent head once more.

The only answer to this is to be systematic. I shall now describe to you a seven-point plan for assembling all the information and weighing up the pros and cons. Like many of the suggestions in this book, it requires pen and paper.

1. Collect together all the scraps of paper, books and notes with your and other people's thoughts, facts and musings on them.
2. Take a large sheet of paper and rule it into three columns. Head these columns PROS, CONS, and UNKNOWN. Write one of the options you are choosing between at the top of the paper, to keep you focused.
3. Go through each of your information sources, taking each item relevant to your decision in turn and jot it down in the appropriate column. Here is an example, showing just part of a 'decision table'.

Decision: To move house now

PROS	CONS	UNKNOWN
Good weather for moving	Middle of school term	House market buoyant
Seen 3 other houses I like	Difficult cashflow	Just bought new carpets
Work not too busy at the moment	Children against it	Pay rise
Garden looks good	Jenny unwell	
Journey to work gets Jenny down	Next door neighbour's house on market	
Monstrous extension next door	Phil says we're crazy	
Row with neighbours	I don't know if I want to move at all	
Jenny hates the kitchen	Cat	
	Are we rushing into this?	
	Emma was born here	

Try to put as few items in UNKNOWNS as possible. This column is for information and opinions which could be either pro or con. Usually it will be possible to place an item as either a definite PRO or a definite CON, however marginally. If they remain in UNKNOWNS they won't be counted at all (see p. 65).

4. When you have listed as many items as you can, take a break! If you can possibly avoid taking a break before this point it is better, because then your judgements about what counts as a PRO and what counts as a CON are more likely to be consistent.

5. The next step is to allocate 'weightings' to each of the items in the three columns. A scale of 1 to 10 is probably adequate, but of course this means your most important, or heavily weighted item can be rated as no more than ten

times as important as the least important item. If your items spread over a much wider range of importance than this, you may need a scale of 1 to 50, or even greater.

The weightings of an item will be decided by two primary factors. First, the more relevant an item is to the decision, the higher a rating you should give it. In our example, Phil's opinion (CON column) may not be very relevant unless he is very close to the family or very informed. The second factor is, quite simply, the importance of an item. The weather (PRO column) is not very important, the decision-maker's feelings about moving (CON column) are more important.

Try to allocate weightings to all the items in one go. Again, your judgements are more likely to be consistent this way.

The items in our example have been allocated weightings below, on a scale of 1 to 10.

Decision: To move house now

PROS		CONS		UNKNOWNS	
Good weather for moving	1	Middle of school term	2	House market buoyant	5
Seen 3 other houses I like	2	Difficult cash-flow	2	Just bought new carpets	3
Work not too busy at the moment	2	Children against it	5	Pay rise	3
Garden looks good	3	Jenny unwell	4		
Journey to work gets Jenny down	7	Next door neighbour's house on market	1		
Monstrous extension next door	4	Phil says we're crazy	1		
Row with neighbours	5	I don't know if I want to move at all	8		
Jenny hates the kitchen	1	Cat	1		
		Are we rushing into this?	8		
		Emma was born here	2		

In our example, the highest weightings are in the CONS column. They have been allocated to items expressing the decision-maker's feelings of unease about moving house now. This illustrates the point that the weightings are intended to be personal, reflecting the decision-maker's view of the importance of these items, not some theoretical objective calculation.

If there are any very high weightings in the UNKNOWNS column, then you should make strenuous efforts to place those items in PROS or CONS, since otherwise they will simply not be taken into account.

6. Now add up the totals for PROS and CONS. If PROS score much higher than CONS, it looks as if the decision you specified at the top of the page is right for you, and vice versa. In our example, PROS score 25, CONS 34. In addition, the two most heavily weighted items are in CONS. It looks as though the decision-maker ought to decide *not* to move house now.

7. If the totals surprise you, look at the items and their weightings again. If the weightings still seem right to you, then the totals are telling you something important that you hadn't realized until you integrated all the disparate items of information. If you change your mind about the weightings, you can play around with them and see how the totals change.

The approach outlined above is a straightforward one. Yet it can be enormously helpful. It need not take longer than an hour or two, and it means you can effectively take into account many more factors than you could juggle in your head at any one time.

Acknowledging what you don't know

However much time and energy you devoted to collecting information, there will be things you wished you knew before you had to make your decision but which you simply could not find out. This may be because the information is too difficult for you to obtain or because no one can know the answer. You can, for example, never predict with complete certainty the emotional consequences for you and other people of particular courses of action or inaction. You can only estimate how external circumstances will change.

Your lists of pros and cons will not be lists of facts, then, but of assessments and guestimates, and there will be gaps. This too you can take into account, at least partially, with your weightings. In the example one of the pros in moving house was 'Row with neighbours'. This was allocated a weighting of 5. That weighting contained a judgement on how serious the effects of that row would be, now and in the future, on the happiness of the family concerned.

Additionally, it may become clear to you as you compile these lists that the things you don't know are fundamental to your decision-making. You need then to reappraise whether you can make the decision yet, and whether you can in fact find out that extra information. You may of course go ahead regardless, but make a note of what you didn't know in your decision diary (Chapter Ten). Later it will be interesting to find out how critical that lack of information turned out to be.

When you are choosing between more than two alternatives

Many decisions will have crystallized into two-alternative decisions by the time you come to weighing up pros and cons. Chapter Two stresses the importance of not taking an either/or view prematurely, but once you have contemplated all the true alternatives, and collected information and advice you will often find your decision is fundamentally whether to take a particular course of action or not. This is after all what decision-making is all about.

Sometimes, however, you are choosing between more than two alternatives at this stage. Perhaps you are buying a house and there are three possibles. Maybe you are fortunate enough to be choosing between four job offers. Clearly you cannot tackle this kind of decision with one column of pros and one of cons. You need pros and cons for each possible choice. The problem is ensuring you are consistent when assessing pros and cons for the different alternatives. You will need to compile all the columns simultaneously. If you have to compile them in two or more goes, include them all each go; don't tackle choice one today and choice two tomorrow.

When you have added up pros and cons for each alternative, subtract the cons from the relevant pros. The alternative with the highest score wins. If cons score higher than pros on all alternatives, then it looks as if you shouldn't be taking any of these courses of action!

The systematic approach does begin to become a little unwieldy as alternatives multiply. So it is better at this stage if you can sensibly frame your decision in terms of whether to take a particular course of action or not. You can always have a series of such two-alternative decisions if a single choice does not do justice to the complexity of the decision. Suppose you are unhappy in your marriage and trying to decide what to do about it. You could tackle this very complex decision as illustrated in simple flow-chart on p. 68, where one of many possible paths is shown.

One of the great values in taking complex decisions a step at a time is that it focuses your mind and stops you worrying about a vast mass of issues all at once. 'Don't cross your bridges before you come to them' is a good maxim in this context. There is no point, to use the example above, in fretting about the impossibility of ever getting your husband to agree to come to marriage guidance before you have even decided whether you truly want to change things. A systematic approach is as useful in mapping out the best course for a complex decision as it is in weighing up the pros and cons of a single course of action.

When the systematic approach is inappropriate

There are some decisions for which the systematic approach is totally inappropriate. It is right for all of the people some of the time, but probably not for any of the people all of the time.

There are decisions which are made in a flash, because there is a single overriding factor which makes only one outcome tolerable. Some friends of mine were looking at houses. The estate agent supplied them with details of one which interested

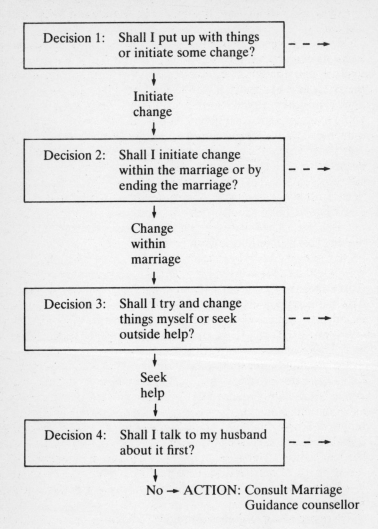

| Decision 1: | Shall I put up with things or initiate some change? | - - → |

Initiate
change

| Decision 2: | Shall I initiate change within the marriage or by ending the marriage? | - - → |

Change
within
marriage

| Decision 3: | Shall I try and change things myself or seek outside help? | - - → |

Seek
help

| Decision 4: | Shall I talk to my husband about it first? | - - → |

No → ACTION: Consult Marriage
Guidance counsellor

them. When they went to look at it, they found it overlooked a cemetery. Since both of them were adamant that they did not want to live right next to a constant reminder of their own mortality, they rejected that house immediately. For decisions like these, the systematic approach would be quite simply a waste of time.

Sometimes there is an overriding factor relevant to a particular decision, but you are not consciously aware of it. What you are likely to find, though, is that when you sit down to try and apply the systematic approach, it won't seem sensible, weightings will appear arbitrary to you, even though you allocated them. You will be tempted to manipulate them to ensure a particular outcome. The systematic approach just will not work.

It is necessary then to go back a step or two. You need to discover the overriding factor so that you can assess its true significance, whether you wish to allow it to determine your decision or not. You may need to consult someone professionally (see Chapter Five) or reflect on your dreams (see Chapter Six).

For decisions like these, the systematic approach does at least highlight that something is going on under the surface, when you try to follow it and find you cannot. A case in point was that of a very bright student, who had just obtained a First Class degree in Economics and was trying to decide whether to do a doctorate or not. She consulted the Careers Officer, took advice from friends in industry, discussed it with her contemporaries. She became very knowledgeable about the effect studying for a doctorate would have on her career prospects, finances, and so on.

She attempted to list the pros and cons in respect of studying for a doctorate or taking a job in industry immediately, but while doing this suddenly realized she had an overwhelming desire to leave the university environment for what she perceived as 'the real world'. In explaining her decision not to take a doctorate to friends subsequently, she always said that she had wanted to 'get her hands dirty'. Her attempts to be systematic had highlighted the strength of her need to do a 'real' job, and once she had recognized that need the systematic approach was no longer relevant.

There are also decisions which have to be made very quickly. Framing the decision and collecting information have to be telescoped into a brief time-scale. There is no time for lists of factors and weightings. Before you make a fast decision, however, ask yourself whether it actually needs to be that fast or whether you are being hurried because it suits someone else. Potential employers often ask for decisions at interview, yet you can always say you will telephone them in a day or two when you have had time to think. No sensible employer would think any the less of you for that.

Having acknowledged that the systematic approach is not appropriate for all decisions, we shall now consider some common arguments against this approach and how valid those arguments are. These arguments are commonly brought to bear against any systematic approach to solving life's problems and complexities, and so they require to be considered in relation to the particular approach we are advocating here.

Argument 1: 'I haven't got time'. This argument is often put forward because of a genuine misunderstanding about how long it takes to put the systematic approach into practice. Writing, summarizing, assessing — these are all activities which sound very time-consuming to practical people. The truth is, however, that the systematic approach can take more or less time, depending on how much time you have. A single evening can be plenty. Indeed, the actual listing and assessing of pros and cons is better done quickly and determinedly rather than in a casual way. Also, the more often you do it, the quicker you become at it, as with most things.

Sometimes arguing that being systematic is too time-consuming is just another way of saying you don't believe the approach is worth it. Then the best thing to do is to try it, just once or twice, and see whether it does help you make a more reasoned decision.

If you can use the systematic approach to control your worrying over a decision, then it can save you time. By this I mean that you consciously allocate in advance a particular evening, weekend, or set of times, for listing and assessing pros and cons. Then, whenever you find yourself beginning to fret about the decision in a general way, you remind yourself that now is not the time for it, that you have saved a space for considering all the factors, and so you can forget about it for the time being and do something else.

Once you have compiled your lists and made your assessments, they are written down for you to refer to at any time. This means you are less likely to go round and round in circles, and again you will save time. It is very common that, when we have a major and difficult decision to make, we are suddenly struck, in the middle of the night, or while having dinner, or sitting in the bath, or whenever, by a 'horrible thought' connected with a possible consequence of the decision.

Fascinated by this horrible thought, we begin to go over in our minds how it might come about, how it might be prevented, how likely it is. Suddenly, as if someone has switched a light on, we remember we have been through this worry, and resolved it before, and we let out a sigh of relief. If we have written out our pros and cons, as soon as the horrible thought strikes us we can refer to our lists and check whether we have already taken it into account or not. This saves us time and spares us emotional exhaustion.

Lastly, if you find yourself thinking 'I haven't got time to do all this', ask yourself how you are in fact going to make your decision. It is unlikely you will make it without spending any time on it at all. Probably you will talk to someone about it, think about it a bit, maybe check through some papers or read a magazine or two. Can you replace any of these activities with a session spent listing and assessing pros and cons? It is harder work but it will pay off.

Argument 2: 'I'm not the analytical type'. There are two main reasons why people bring this argument to bear. One is that they are quite simply daunted by the prospect of listing factors and allocating values. The activity appears rather intellectual and academic, far removed from the ordinary business of living. The other is that they are actually contemptuous of pencil and paper, of logic and system. They consider that their lives run perfectly satisfactorily without any introspection or analysis.

This second group of people will not find the systematic approach helpful. It is truly at odds with their way of living. It would not be sensible to urge them to tack it on to their normal intuitive lifestyle. If they become dissatisfied with the quality of

71

their decision-making, if they begin to feel that things are not on the whole turning out the way they intended them to, then they might like to try the approach advocated in this book. Otherwise, listing pros and cons and assigning numerical values are probably inappropriate activities for them.

Many people, however, would like to be more systematic. System and order imply control, and, as we discussed right back in Chapter One, control over your own life is a good thing. Many of those who would like to be more systematic are afraid that they do not have the intellectual powers. The systematic approach intimidates them. It appears to be for 'clever people' and they don't consider themselves to be clever.

There are two things to say about this. The first is that most of us are much cleverer than we realize. Think of it as walking and running. Most of the time, when we go on foot from one place to another, we walk. Even if we walk ninety-five per cent of the time, that does not mean we cannot run. We don't run, generally, because it is more effort and usually unnecessary. But when we have to, we can run, and most of us can run quite fast. In the same way, we are on the whole as clever as we need to be. Most of life's demands can be met adequately with the intellectual equivalent of walking. But we can draw on extra resources of cleverness when we need to. The resources are there. We just have to recognize when we do need to, and have the confidence to draw on those resources.

I would argue that for this last stage of decision-making, weighing up the pros and cons, we have to run a little. It is difficult to bear in mind all the conflicting requirements and outcomes, to set aside unreasoned bias, to balance one factor against another, and to imagine how things might turn out for better or worse. It is difficult, but it is well within the intellectual ability of most of us. Often we cannot do it because we cannot face it emotionally, and we have already talked about how frightening decision-making can be (Chapter One). But I am sure we are intellectually capable of the task.

The second thing to say is that the systematic approach does not require abstract intellectual skills. Neither does it require knowledge of maths, philosophy or formal logic. The kind of

72

cleverness it requires is organized common-sense. If you have collected information in the way described in Chapter Three, listing the factors is straightforward. You need to be thorough, able to summarize the essence of the information and reasonably quick at doing so. Assigning values to the factors is more difficult, but more because it requires you to be imaginative and consistent, rather than because it requires you to be scientific in an academic way. This level of analytical skill is within the reach of most of us, if we want it to be.

Argument 3: 'It's all too cold-blooded'. This argument is partly valid, in that it recognizes that a primary objective of the systematic approach is to control the strong emotional responses most of us have to any major decision. A fundamental assumption of the whole approach is that uncontrolled emotion leads to poor decision-making. In fact, few would dispute this.

Some would argue, however, that the systematic approach takes things too far. It strips human decisions of humanity, pretends people can calculate and assess like machines, and offers a starkly mechanical solution to life's crisis points.

To argue like this is to misunderstand how the approach is to be applied. It will be recalled that earlier in this chapter we stressed in the example that emotions and gut feelings are an important, if not the most important, basis for allocating weightings. Emotions are taken into account, they are given a high priority, but this is done in an open, ordered way. Emotional reasons are acknowledged as such. They may in the end decide the question, but they will do so explicitly. When decisions are made unsystematically, the decision-makers are often at the mercy of their emotions. They may not even know that it is fear, guilt or greed driving them towards a particular decision. With the systematic approach, they can still allow fear, guilt or greed to determine their decision, but they will have chosen to do so.

There is a slightly different but related argument against the systematic approach. It is that we are at the mercy of our emotions, whatever we do, and we are just deceiving ourselves if we imagine any strategy or approach can alter this. This argument is also related to the fatalistic arguments we considered in Chapter Two, and as with those arguments I shall not attempt to disprove it here. It is certainly worth trying to gain some control over our emotions; it is certainly difficult to do so. I believe it is possible but naturally others are free to believe the contrary.

Argument 4: 'It's too boring'. The first counter-argument to the case that the systematic approach is boring is that the approach is very important. In some senses, whether it is boring or exciting is irrelevant, since it is fundamental to effective decision-making and, as we have discussed extensively elsewhere, effective decision-making is one of the keys to ensuring your life turns out the way you want it. You may find sleep or work boring, but nevertheless you will both sleep and work.

I think it is true that aspects of the systematic approach are boring, in the sense that they are hard work with no instant pay-offs. Listing all the factors is one such aspect, although as the lists grow and you begin to perceive for the first time the balance between pros and cons, the job becomes more interesting. If you are making a decision jointly with someone else, finding out their pros and cons also adds to the interest, as does negotiating the weightings subsequently.

On balance, the argument that the systematic approach is too boring doesn't hold. If you find you are bored with it while using it you may be using it to tackle too trivial decisions. Alternatively, you may have collected too much detailed information and so can't see the wood for the trees. Stand back from your lists and reconsider.

8

Joint decision-making:
Usefulness of the Systematic Approach

The key characteristic of a joint decision is that two or more people have equal responsibility, rights and involvement in making it. A classic example is a married couple's decision whether to move house. Parent's decisions on their children's upbringing and education are common joint decisions. Joint decisions may also be made by groups of friends, business associates, or colleagues. A joint decision is quite different from a decision taken by a single individual with advice from others. In that case, the outcome of the decision will not affect the advisers, or will affect them only marginally. A joint decision affects all those making it to a comparable degree.

Problems with Joint Decisions, and Systematic Solutions

A major difficulty with a joint decision lies in ensuring that each person involved in making it does actually have a fair, if not scrupulously equal, say. If the decision is left to a lot of informal discussion and argument, in practice the more forceful personality will probably make the decision. Another major difficulty is that of avoiding too much conflict and bad feeling between the joint decision-makers. Again, informality allows heated and often very counter-productive disputes to escalate until none of the parties is thinking rationally or sensitively. Then again, when two or more people bring their preferences, knowledge and ideas to the 'decision table', it is extremely difficult to keep track of all the pros and cons they raise, and to incorporate them all in the decision-making process.

The solution to these three major difficulties can be found in the systematic approach to weighing up pros and cons advocated here. It is at this point in the decision-making process that decisions can become truly joint. All of the earlier stages, from asking the right question to collecting information to taking advice, can be done independently by all those involved in the decision. Indeed, there is a lot to be said for everyone going off on their own decision trail, for a greater variety of information and approaches will then ensue. When it comes to weighing up the pros and cons, however, the decision-makers must join together and work as a team, if they wish to achieve a truly joint decision. We shall now examine how the systematic approach enables them to do this.

Joint decisions and listing the factors

The three lists, of pros and cons and unknowns, can be compiled using the information, views and experience of all the decision-makers. The aim of these lists is to provide a comprehensive appraisal of the factors affecting the decision. Two or more people working together to compile them are likely to produce a much more comprehensive list than one person on his own. At this stage, there is no need to argue about whether a pro or con should be on the list; they can all be included and their importance reflected subsequently in the weightings attached to them. Of course, there may be disagreement as to whether an individual factor counts as a pro or a con. In discussing the choice of State or private education for a child, for example, one parent may consider the relative egalitarianism of the State system to be an advantage, while the other considers it a disadvantage. In cases like this, the factor can quite simply be included in both the pro and the con column. Then, again at the weighting stage, the decision-makers may jointly assess it to be a more important pro than con, or vice versa. Or the same value will be attached to it in each column and it will be cancelled out.

Alternatively, the decision-makers may realize that the factor itself is too general to be a useful input to their decision, and may break it down into more specific components. In the example we have mentioned concerning egalitarianism of a State school vis à vis a public school, the parent who regards this as a pro for choosing a State school may recognize that it is the opportunity for the child to mix on equal terms with children from many different backgrounds that they particularly value. The parent who regards it as a con may recognize that it is the risk of their child being treated anonymously that they particularly fear.

One of the great merits in listing everyone's pros and cons together is that this exercise in itself promotes communication and understanding between the decision-makers. This is why it is important not to weed out any factors at this stage but to include them all. This stage is on the whole intended to be a non-contentious one, all parties having the common objective of obtaining as full a set of lists as possible. In that atmosphere it is possible to take in the viewpoint of your decision-making partner, to listen to their pros and cons without feeling you are losing ground. Don't fall into the trap of only listing pros, or only cons, while your partner does the opposite. That will put you straight into contention and dispute, and that is better left to the weighting stage.

The importance of taking a break

You will recall that after you have finished the lists you should take a break. This is even more important if you are making a joint decision. The listing and the weighting stages are fundamentally different in terms of how you work together, and a break will help to underline that difference.

Joint decisions and weighting the factors

I have already touched on the fact that it is at the weighting stage that discussion and dispute can begin. You must arrive at an agreed weighting for each factor, and that is difficult. Now, the great strength of this approach is that it ties the discussion down to specific points. You should try very hard to keep to the point when discussing the weighting for an individual factor, in order to exploit this strength. Joint decisions often break down because the decision-makers return to the same old fundamental disagreement over and over again, nearly always at a very general level. The lists you have compiled give you an agenda for your discussion, and a very detailed one at that.

The other great advantage of going through the factors one by one is that it will become painfully obvious if one of the decision-makers is a bully or a passenger. If it is always the same one who allots the final weighting, then it is transparently clear that this is no true joint decision. Even the bully may begin to feel a little embarrassed!

Joint decisions and adding up

Once the weightings have been allocated, adding up is non-contentious. And the outcome, both in terms of whether pros or cons score higher and of how large the difference is, can easily surprise all parties. Whether you stick to the outcome or not is up to you, but if you have worked through the systematic approach together in the way I have just described it is likely to be the closest to a joint decision that you will come.

Finally, a word in praise of joint decisions. They probably seem like a lot of hard work, and it's tempting to wonder if they're worth it. Perhaps it would be better just to hand each decision over to one person. The problem with that is that person then has too much responsibility and power. He can be blamed and isolated if things turn out badly, admired and isolated if they turn out well. Joint decisions are the building blocks of joint enterprise, ranging from marriage to parenting to starting a business. They are difficult and time-consuming, but without them we could never truly share any part of our lives with anyone else.

9

Decisive Decision-making: How to Know When You've Made Up Your Mind

It is common to admire so-called 'decisive' people. Sometimes, however, what is taken for 'decisiveness' is in fact bigotry or arrogance. As the first seven chapters of this book have emphasized, fast inflexible decision-making based on little or biased information-gathering is not to be recommended. There is a danger, however, in the systematic and measured approach I have advocated up to now. It is that your decision-making style will swing to the opposite extreme and that you will be a ditherer. So this chapter is concerned with true decisiveness. It assumes you have gathered and assessed information in the ways the previous chapters describe. It addresses the question of knowing when to stop. It takes as its central theme the importance of identifying and exploiting the deadlines attached to the decisions which face you.

A positive approach to deadlines

First, let us consider those decisions which impose their own time-scale. You may have to make a decision within a set time, anything from minutes to years: a time-driven decision. Alternatively, you may have to decide by the time something else takes place, at present due to occur at some indeterminate future time: an event-driven decision. I shall refer to decisions such as these as having an 'external' time-scale, that is, external to you, the decision-maker, the deadline being to a large extent out of your control.

At least such decisions provide a framework for your decision-making. There's nothing like a set time-limit to focus the mind. I would see the deadline as something useful to be exploited rather than something to be bemoaned. If the time-limit is anything longer than a couple of minutes, arrange your different decision-making activities within the set time, moving on to the next stage as soon as time runs out.

This is how I approach choosing exam questions, for example. Five minutes can be spared in selecting a question, no longer: two minutes to scan the paper and tick possibles, two minutes to study the possibles and select one, one minute to check that that one has no subtle implications to tape your ignorance. (Of course, practice makes the whole process less daunting.) Exceptionally, I would then have to overrun that time limit, discard the first choice, and select another possibility.

Once you see a deadline in this positive way, you will tend to look for external time-scales in all decisions you have to make. Usually people avoid facing up to deadlines providing they are sufficiently far away, because they find them frightening. This is the 'if you ignore it long enough, it will go away' approach.

One of the many bad consequences of this approach for effective decision-making is that the deadline arrives without your having used any of the intervening time to gather information, take advice, or assess the evidence. Sometimes, maybe often, we behave like this so that we can have an excuse for making a decision without thinking. 'I didn't realize the applications had to be in by tomorrow; I'll leave it.' Sometimes we do it to avoid taking responsibility for the decision we want to make. 'It's so late, I can't visit him now.' 'If only I had remembered to phone the restaurant earlier.'

There may be good reasons for behaving like this, and at times those reasons may outweigh your desire to engage in effective decision-making. It is with effective decision-making that this book is concerned, however, and the golden rules for managing deadlines are clear:

> Find out what the deadline is.
> Plan how to use the time available.
> Stick to the plan.
> Once the deadline is past, don't go back.

The last rule requires some explanation. Out of context, it could sound over-rigid, as if you had to stick with a bad decision when it was clear you could change things. There is a distinction to be made, however, between changing your mind after the deadline is past, and making further decisions which will alter the consequences of a bad decision.

How to avoid appearing to dither

Suppose, for example, you have applied for a job and sent the application off. Almost as soon as you have put the application in the post, you realize you do not want the job at all. This may, by the way, be a sign that your decision-making was ineffective or alternatively that the decision was one of those rare ones where you can only see things clearly once you have taken an irrevocable step.

However that may be, what do you do now? The ditherer will ring the company he has applied to and withdraw the application, or sit and bite his nails hoping, ironically, not to be offered the job. The effective decision-maker, on the other hand, will contact the company he has applied to, and give a plausible, and possibly but not necessarily true, account of why he doesn't feel able/ready/experienced enough to take the job yet, and discuss possible future openings. He will do this after his application has been received. He will thus not be dithering over whether to apply or not. He will have accepted that his decision to apply was final; now he is altering the use he makes of his application. Not only is this a more constructive use of his time and energy, but also, just as importantly, he is seen as confident, constructive and decisive by the outside world. It is at least as vital to be seen to be decisive as actually to be decisive, but more of that later.

Imposing your own deadline

We turn now from the relatively clear guidelines for decisions with external time-scales to the muddier waters of decisions which could theoretically, and sometimes do, drag on for ever, or at least for a very long time. These are decisions where you have a large amount of freedom in choosing when to make up your mind.

Again, if you want to make a lifetime's hobby out of avoiding decisions, that's up to you, but in that case you should either put this book down now or start again at the beginning. There are plenty of people who stay in their jobs, their homes, their marriages, purely because they have never got round to deciding to leave.

For the aspiring effective decision-maker, decisions with primarily internal time-scales pose a problem. All other things being equal, the more quickly a decision can be made, the better. There is more time then to enjoy the consequences, and to move on to the next thing. Yet all other things are not equal. Gathering information takes time. So does assessing it. Testing your own reactions in different moods and circumstances (see Chapter Six) also requires time. You have to identify your own deadline at a point in time which maximizes the potential benefits of your decisions and minimizes the risk of overlooking a vital factor.

I think that it is helpful to draw a picture to identify that deadline. The kind of picture I am going to describe needs to be no more than a rough sketch. It is not a precise, mathematical graph although it is a graph-type drawing. It enables you to map, against time, what you have to gain and lose at different points from making the decision, and how well equipped you will be to make it then. First draw a line to indicate an approximate feasible maximum time-scale. Here are two examples:

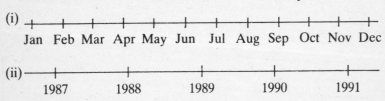

Then draw a line to indicate how much of the potential relevant information, of all kinds, you are likely to have at different points in that time-scale:

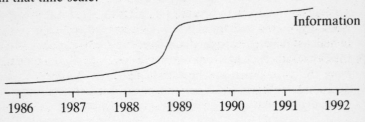

Finally draw a line to indicate the potential benefits of the right decision throughout the time-scale:

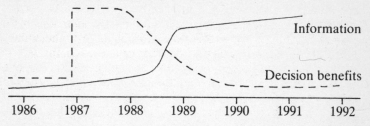

Then you can identify, approximately at least, the optimum time at which to make your decision. You should have as much information as you can, given that you do not want to delay too long, and where possible you want the potential benefits of a correct decision at that time to be high.

I shall now draw out the lines for making a decision on whether to have your child vaccinated against whooping cough, a vaccination which carries a very slight risk of brain damage to some children. This is the kind of decision parents worry over for years, if they cannot make up their minds to have their child vaccinated. The lines look something like this, for a child born in 1982:

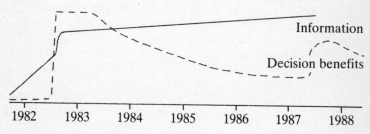

To explain the decision benefits line first, the vaccination is not normally offered until the child is six months old, so the potential benefits of making the right decision come in at that point. Since the risks both of death from whooping cough and brain damage from the vaccination are highest in the first year of life, the decision benefits line is at its peak here. The potential benefits decline gradually after the first year as the child's strength and natural resistance to disease increase. At school age, potential benefits increase once more, as the child is more likely to become infected as a result of his increased social contact and the consequences of contracting the illness include missing school as well as purely physical effects.

The information line assumes that most information about the likely consequences of both vaccination and non-vaccination is available to you by the end of the child's first year. A lot of information will be available at six months, when the vaccination is offered. You are likely to find out a little bit more as the years go by, case histories of children you know, the odd bit of scientific research reported in the press, but it is improbable that any major new factor will come to your attention after the end of the first year.

So in this case the decision lines suggest that the point which maximizes the potential benefits and minimizes the risk of overlooking a vital factor is when your child is about 7 months old. It would be sensible to make a decision one way or the other at that point and stick to it. If you make the 'reversible' decision, that is, not to have your child vaccinated, of course you may reverse it if some major new information of relevance comes to your attention, or if a sudden change in circumstances alters your previous assessment of information. If you make the 'irreversible' decision, you can be confident you did so at the right time and in your child's best interests.

So drawing decision lines can help you know when to decide, and thus avoid your contracting inadvertently the other sort of decision lines—the facial furrows you develop when you can't make up your mind!

Is there life after deadlines?

There is one final point to be made in the context of deadlines. Clearly none of us can make decisions which we can guarantee to last for ever. We may, for example, decide to live in the country in 1984 and to live in the town in 1987. We may decide to pursue a career in advertising when we leave university, and change to teaching five years later. So there is a delicate distinction to be drawn between chopping and changing, and revising a decision when appropriate.

One way to guard against sensible change turning into vacillation is to attach time-limits to your decisions when you make them. The decision is seen as 'running out' at the end of the time allotted. You might, for example, decide to stay in your present job for at least two years. You would define your time-limit not arbitrarily but for sensible reasons, such as ensuring your C.V. looks presentable, behaving in a reasonable way towards your employers, allowing yourself time to do other things than job-hunt. With a time-limit like this attached, your decision would then stand for two years. At the end of that time you would review it.

The good thing about attaching these time-limits at the time you make a decision is that you are likely to be able to assess reasonably calmly the right length of time to let the decision stand. Then, when you arrive home after an argument with your boss, fully intending to hand in your notice the next day, you will at least have to take into account the time-limit you had attached to your decision to take the job in the first place!

Keeping up appearances

I have already mentioned that it is at least as vital to be seen to be decisive as actually to be decisive. This is for several reasons. Firstly, and quite simply, because people in general believe decisiveness to be a good quality. So if you allow others to label you as a ditherer, you will be less respected. Secondly, if it is clear that you stick by your decisions, other people will know where they are. They can then act on your decisions, offer you help, adjust their own expectations, and so on. If you have a reputation for changing your mind as often as you change your socks, those around you are eventually forced to ignore your decisions. If they were to take you seriously, they would run the risk of being embarrassed and misled. An example will perhaps illustrate how one individual's indecisiveness can create enormous problems for those around him.

A case study in dithering. Tim was a teacher in a secondary school. He enjoyed his work, but considered the salary too low. He wondered whether he should leave teaching and pursue a career in industry.

Tim went to discuss things with his headmaster. His headmaster was helpful and positive, outlined for Tim what his career prospects were likely to be in teaching and in his school in particular. He offered Tim some additional administrative responsibilities which brought with them a slight increase in salary. Tim felt much happier after this discussion, took on the extra responsibilities, and told his family and friends he had decided to stay in teaching.

Some weeks later, Tim and his wife saw a house for sale which they liked very much and would have bought if they had been able to afford it. Tim became restless again about his job. He talked about it to his wife, and with his colleagues, and was again persuaded that the extra income was not so important. Meanwhile, it had come to the headmaster's attention that Tim was thinking again about leaving. He felt let down and annoyed, and began to wonder whether he would have to find someone else to take over Tim's responsibilities.

Then Tim saw a job advertised in the national press which appealed to him. He applied, and was called for interview. He had to ask his headmaster for time off for the interview. His colleagues and family were jettisoned once more into a state of uncertainty. Tim was in fact offered the job but turned it down on consideration. The firm he had applied to were not impressed with his dithering. There was in addition a feeling amongst some of Tim's colleagues that it might have been better if he had left.

Tim could not come to terms with having turned the job down. He discussed the pros and cons with his wife, his parents, friends and colleagues. His wife felt anxious: Tim did not seem settled but she could not think how to help him. They would have a discussion which appeared to reach a resolution, Tim would seem happy for a while, then a few days later he would bring the subject up again, with her or with other people. Tim's colleagues began to grow impatient. They had given a lot of time to Tim, and yet he seemed no nearer a final decision.

Tim went to see a firm of career consultants in London. He was very excited about their assessment of him initially. They had apparently unearthed evidence of entrepreneurial flair. He was impressed by their qualifications and experience, and told everyone he now understood what kind of job he should be looking for. His family and friends felt resentful that he had sought advice from all of them, and then apparently ignored it in favour of some distant expert who didn't know Tim half as well as they did.

There is no end to this story. Tim is still teaching and still contemplating leaving. His indecisiveness has resulted in the following problems for those who know him.

- His headmaster has given Tim extra responsibility but has no assurance that Tim will stay.
- The stability of his school has been undermined.
- His wife cannot plan, nor devote much attention to her own career prospects. Tim has a monopoly on domestic unease.
- His colleagues feel devalued. Tim is not committed to them nor to what they are trying to achieve in the school.
- All those who have given Tim advice feel they have wasted their breath.

How you can appear decisive

Even if Tim could not actually decide once and for all whether to stay in teaching or not, there are a number of simple principles he could have followed to ensure he at least appeared decisive.

1. Tim gave the impression that he was 'always' agonizing over his career. Mentioning any one decision frequently, over a long period, always in the same terms, soon leads people to believe you to be indecisive. Never say 'I can't decide'. Say 'I haven't decided yet'. Better still, say 'Ask me next week/month/term. I shall decide this week-end/at the end of the month/in the holidays.' Statements like these give the impression you are working to a plan, rather than aimlessly pondering.

2. Tim discussed his decision with everyone he knew. This is a mistake. Reserve serious discussions about a decision for people who can truly help you to make the right

decision. Ask people only those questions they can reasonably be expected to answer informatively (see Chapter Four).

3. Tim listened to his wife's advice, but went over the same ground again with other people in front of her. Not only will this kind of behaviour make you appear indecisive, it will also annoy the person whose advice you first took. Unless you make it clear that their advice has contributed to your understanding and moved you on to the next stage of decision-making, they will feel their advice has been discarded. Don't ask the same questions over and over again, and if you must go over exactly the same points with more than one person, do it discreetly.

4. If you know you have not made up your mind yet, don't allow people to take action as if you had. Tim should not have taken on the extra responsibilities his headmaster offered since he knew he was still contemplating leaving teaching in the short term. Be clear and honest. Say 'Don't do anything about this yet—I'll let you know when I've finally decided.' People understand that some decisions take a long time to make. What they object to is not so much waiting as being led up the garden path.

5. There is no need to go public on a decision prematurely. People are nearly always less interested in the details of your life than you imagine them to be. Tell those who need to know when they need to know. Tell those who are interested when they ask.

6. Discriminate explicitly between more and less serious decisions. If you treat deciding whether to paint the living-room green or blue with the same weight as deciding whether to move house you will quickly acquire the reputation of a ditherer. Sometimes, make a point of deciding a fairly trivial matter on the spur of the moment. At other times, say that a particular decision is going to need thinking about. This will give people the impression that you only spend time on a decision when it is necessary and not as a result of some character flaw.

7. Vary the confidence with which you announce your decisions. If you always claim your decision to be

88

definitely right, you will be discounted, quite rightly, as arrogant. If you always qualify your decision with 'I'm not sure if this is the right thing but. . . .' then you will certainly not be seen as decisive. When you are confident, say so. When not, admit to some doubts, but make it clear that your decision is based on your best understanding and that it needed to be made. Tell people the time-limits attached to particular decisions, if there are any. If you have planned to review a decision after two years, when you do so you will be seen as organized, not dithering.

8. If you really need to change your mind, try to represent the change as progress, rather than a simple U-turn. Say 'I've just thought of a slightly better way to tackle this' or 'Let's not only do such-and-such but also so-and-so'. Let a little time elapse before you reverse a decision, and then say 'I've been thinking about things. We didn't consider something important and it sheds a new light on things.' Even with this approach, you must stick to a decision once made much more often than you reverse one.

9. It can be better to make a possibly bad decision decisively and move on rather than spend lots of time debating it. People's memories are short, and provided you do actually move on and don't spend time on post-mortems and regrets you will usually carry them with you. A colleague of mine resigned, only to find his new employers on the verge of bankruptcy. He immediately applied for lots more jobs with great energy and enthusiasm, got another job within a month, which was better paid than his first, and never looked back. Neither did his friends, who soon could not even remember the somewhat inauspicious circumstances which led to his applying for his current job.

10. Finally, if you are sure you have made a bad mistake, don't sacrifice your happiness or security just for the sake of appearing decisive. All other things being equal, to appear decisive is a good thing, but if you've left home and heartily wish you hadn't, if you've given up work to look after your children and it's driving you crazy, or if

you've booked a holiday you know you won't enjoy, then other considerations than how decisive you appear are paramount. People who acknowledge they have made mistakes are respected. It's just that people who make too many are suspected of bad management.

The two keys to true decisiveness

To return now to the reality from the appearance, there are two qualities you need to cultivate in order to become truly decisive. The first is imagination. The second is discipline. Lots of people have one or the other of these, but both are required for effective decision-making.

You use your imagination to understand as fully as you can how your decision might work out in practice. The mother of a two year old who is contemplating moving to the country must imagine what her decision will mean when her child is of school age, and when he is a thoroughly sociable teenager. The confirmed bachelor contemplating marriage will need all his resources of imagination, and more, to foresee how every detail of his life will change. In all decisions, the more imaginatively you can approach them, the more able you will be to make a decision you can stick to in the future.

Discipline is what you need to progress from early uncertainty to a point where you know what to do. You will face up to and assess the implications your imagination has enabled you to identify. You will stop when the deadline arrives. You will plan who to talk to and when.

Of course, much of this book up to now has been concerned with practical ways you can cultivate both imagination and discipline in your decision-making. For it is not easy to be decisive. In a world of uncertainty, where at any time something totally unexpected may happen, it is one of the most difficult qualities to achieve.

10

Asymmetric Decisions:
How Not to Take the Path of
Least Resistance

A decision is asymmetric when one of the possible choices will happen anyway, by default, if you don't do anything to prevent it. The other choices will only happen if you do something positive. Many major decisions are asymmetric in this sense. An obvious example is moving house. If you don't move, you will stay in the same house. You don't appear to have decided to stay; you have just not decided to move. Changing jobs is similar—so is changing anything.

The problem with these asymmetric decisions is that they encourage us to allow the course of our lives to drift on, without our taking positive charge. This is just another way in which we see that change requires effort. The path of least resistance makes a detour round active decision-making, and we don't even have to choose the path consciously. We just find ourselves on it.

Why not take the path of least resistance? Here are some reasons.

Lost opportunities
If you don't consciously weigh up alternatives to different aspects of your life, you may miss opportunities of great value. The times to be particularly watchful in this regard are times when you are about to take a step which is likely to commit you to a particular course for some time. Leaving school is one such time, getting engaged or married another, taking a new job another. Pause for a brief moment to consider what else you could do. If your planned course of action is sound, it will stand up to a little examination. If it is not, better to find out now than later.

Often a decision made a long time go has started some ball rolling, things happen which suggest you should change course but the momentum is too great, and you just take the path of least resistance. You can of course decide to change later, but it is much better before you have invested too much in an unwise choice.

A friend of mine had a holiday romance in Australia. She and the man she had met decided to get married. She returned to England to work her notice, and after about six months her fiancé flew over for the wedding. They were going to make their home in Australia, where he had a profitable business. Relatives from two continents had gathered for the wedding, the church was booked, the wedding dress made and all the presents bought. Two days before the wedding my friend cancelled it. Her growing unease had developed into certainty that she could not face that degree of upheaval on the basis of a few months' knowledge of this man. They may marry in the future, but there is no guarantee.

She had a great deal of courage to defy that rolling ball of expectation, family pressure, inevitability. I often think of her when I am tempted by the path of least resistance.

Vague discontent

If you don't actively choose how you want to live your life, you will not make the most of what you have. Even if you choose the path of least resistance, providing you choose it rather than just drifting down it, you are much less likely to succumb to vague and ineffectual discontent.

Let me illustrate this point. You are not happy in your job. You are always meaning to apply for another, but never get round to it. So you stay in the same job, feeling vaguely discontented for years. Suppose, instead, you had decided to choose whether and when to change jobs. Even if you decided to stay, your attitude would change. If you decided to stay indefinitely you would be doing so for positive reasons. You would be likely to make the most of it. Having admitted you were not leaving, you would take steps to change the things that you didn't like, as far as possible. If you decided to stay for a period of time, and then apply for other jobs, you would have a goal to work towards.

If you don't change, having examined the alternatives, you have not taken the path of least resistance. You have chosen not to change. Vive la différence.

Invitation to manipulation

If you habitually take the path of least resistance, you invite other people to manipulate you. They soon discover that by arranging things for you, by making certain courses of action easier than others, they can exert enormous influence over you. The techniques used by high pressure salesmen are based on this weakness in human nature. They attempt to set up a situation where inactivity implies acquiescence and results in a sale. Seduction can also follow the same principle successfully. Little by little, a situation is established where to have sex is the 'most natural thing in the world'.

To be sold a washing-machine or a brief affair on the basis of such manipulation is perhaps not serious. To allow your life to be determined by the schemers of this world certainly is, although it must be said that some people find this a genuinely attractive solution to the problems and anxieties they would otherwise face. Those people, however, won't be reading this book.

How to approach asymmetric decisions

I am not advocating that we should all live in a state of constant turmoil, questioning every aspect of our lives continuously so as to be sure we are not taking the path of least resistance unthinkingly. To behave like that would certainly not be in the interests of effective decision-making. What we can do is identify 'points' and 'pointers' which mark a time when we should re-examine fundamentals.

Points at which to focus on asymmetric decisions

We have already mentioned one point when it is a good idea to challenge a path we are set on. That is when we are about to make a major step which will commit us definitely for some considerable time.

Another point is when an opportunity arises which you hadn't expected. A colleague of mine was 'headhunted' recently by a firm he had had some minor dealings with. This came totally out of the blue, and he was tempted to dismiss the approach without much thought. Recognizing it as a significant opportunity which deserved greater consideration, however, he sat down and considered the pros and cons of leaving his job versus the pros and cons of staying. He used this external and unexpected event as a trigger to reassessment.

Another very common point is when something happens in your family or circle of close friends which possibly necessitates some action on your part. A relative becomes ill, for example, and then you may wish to reassess where you live in the light of that. Would you like to live closer, so as to be of more help? Would you like to live further away, so as not to be expected to help? After all, we make the best decisions we can in the circumstances which prevail; if the circumstances change, it is sensible to review the decisions.

Another point is when you learn something important you had never thought of before. In Chapter Three, on collecting information, we recognized that you can't know everything before you make a decision. This means that sometimes new relevant information will come to light which requires you to reassess a past decision. The new information has to be quite significant, however. You might, for example, be engaged to be married, and during your engagement discover aspects of your fiancé's character you find rather disturbing. Perhaps you begin to see that he is mean with money, or ruthless towards individuals with whom he has financial dealings. This inform-ation should lead you to reassess your decision to marry him, although it will take courage. As we have discussed before, knowing when you've made up your mind entails accepting that further information might come to light but that you gain more by deciding now than by hanging on, indefinitely.

In the previous chapter, the possibility of attaching time-limits to particular decisions was discussed. Whenever a decision 'runs out', that is a point for reappraisal. Of course, you will need to keep a record of these time-limits if you are to take action when they expire. (The next chapter, on 'Decision Diaries') will help you here.

Pointers which indicate your asymmetric decisions require attention

We have considered some clearly identifiable points at which you should attend to asymmetric decisions. They are all essentially to do with something happening, the outside world or your knowledge changing, or time running out. There is another category of indices that you may have taken a wrong turning onto the path of least resistance. These are 'pointers' rather than 'points', gut feelings and patterns of individually insignificant occurrences which can alert you to the need for change.

Pain Just as physical pain draws our attention to damage to our body which requires healing, so emotional pain draws our attention to a need for change in our lives. I would include under the heading 'pain' feelings of unease, apprehension, discontent and envy as well as anguish proper. These feelings are pointers which should alert us that it is time to make a change. Usually we know what area of our lives is causing the trouble; occasionally we honestly don't, and then we need to consult a professional (see Chapter Five). In a way, emotional pain turns what was the path of least resistance into a path of considerable resistance, although even so it is surprising how many people stick with bad decisions and the resulting pain rather than risk change.

It is well known that certain kinds of physical malady are also pointers to a need to reappraise our lives. Common examples are stomach disorders, headaches, palpitations and skin complaints.

People Our family, friends and acquaintances can give us useful pointers to a need for change. Sometimes, good-humoured teasing can suggest to us we are rather stuck in our ways. A friend will say 'Oh, you always complain but you'll never leave that job' and suddenly we realize they may be right. Or you notice that things are being planned on the assumption that you will still be doing x, y and z in two years time.

Ask yourself whether you are seen as someone whose life may

develop in unexpected and interesting ways or rather as 'good old so-and-so'. Do people think of you as a drifter or a dynamo? You probably don't want to be either. Although people's perceptions of you are invariably clouded by their own pre-occupations, they can still assist you by indicating when you might profitably review an asymmetric decision or two.

Plus ça change, plus c'est la même chose It is appropriate here, in a chapter where we are considering decision-making as a means of bringing about constructive change, to point out a particular way in which making changes can be deceptive. Suppose you look back over your life and can say with some satisfaction that you have definitely not followed the path of least resistance, you have reviewed all major decisions regularly, you have moved house five times in the last twenty years, changed jobs four times and lived with three different men. It may be that each of the changes was productive, in the sense that your life progressed and you developed as a person. On the other hand, it could be that all the external changes hid the fact that your life was actually going round and round in circles.

We all know other people who repeat patterns in their lives, such as the friend who starts every job enthusiastically, becomes disillusioned with the boss after a few months, and leaves on bad terms declaring she will never work for a company like that again. In fact, we all tend to repeat patterns, and it is for this reason that certain kinds of change can be deceptive. Instead of changing something fundamental about our own attitude or behaviour, we change the situation, frequently. Then, para-doxically, change itself becomes the path of least resistance. So watch out for the fact that the most difficult decision for you might be not to change anything and that deciding not to take action is at least as positive as deciding to act.

Decision-makers who believe in magic

Have you ever heard anyone say any of the following?

'I find decisions usually make themselves, don't you?'
'I don't consciously think about decisions, I just end up doing

96

the right thing.'
'Life always seems to work itself out all right in the end.'

I call the people who say this sort of thing the 'magical' people. They imply that there is some magic, some mystery going on in their lives which guides their decision-making without their conscious participation. They turn taking the path of least resistance into a positive virtue.

I think this is a risky approach, for the following reasons among others:

1. If you accept whatever happens to you as being for the best, you will never find out what other alternatives there might be. You are enmeshed in a self-fulfilling prophecy, which may be very comfortable, but which will limit you and lose you opportunities.
2. 'Magical' people are very frustrating for those of us who don't believe in magic. Certainly, a magical and non-magical person could never make a joint decision.
3. Selfish and unscrupulous people will exploit another's belief in magic to get their own way without being challenged.
3. You will never learn from past decisions, because your rôle is essentially passive.
5. Often people believe in magic out of fear. Making decisions is so terrifying to them that they switch off completely. Yet they will never overcome their fear, unless they begin to take charge.

Since the whole of this book is about *making* decisions and not about letting decisions *happen* to you, it is obvious that I would not recommend a magical approach. There are some people who pretend to believe in magic so that they cannot be held responsible for their decisions, nor be expected to do any work towards making decisions, and others who pretend to believe in magic because they consider it gives them an edge over us earth-bound mortals. Since these people have at least decided to behave in this way, they are a small step further down the road to effective decision-making than the genuine believers.

11

Decision Diaries:
How to Learn from Past Decisions

It is said that a good air traffic controller has the ability to put decisions he has just made, and their consequences, completely out of his mind. He is not then distracted from his immediate task, which requires complete concentration, by memories of near misses, overwhelming feelings of relief or a build-up of excessive confidence.

For effective decision-making in everyday life, however, it is necessary to combine decisiveness with the ability to reflect.

How to learn from past decisions

You need, for example, to begin to find out how effective a decision-maker you already are. I know people who say that they are hopeless at making decisions but in fact lead very planned and organized lives. Perhaps they are good at making decisions but don't realize their own strengths. Conversely, there are those who are over-confident in their decision-making ability, who constantly change their minds but fool themselves into believing they just hadn't finished deciding until now.

Companies will hire management consultants to assess how effectively their executives make business decisions; we cannot afford to hire anyone else to study our personal decision-making so we have to find a way of doing it for ourselves.

Reflection on past decisions can follow on naturally from the decision-making process advocated in this book. If you have started to make your decisions consciously and actively, to collect and assess information systematically, and to identify decision deadlines, then it is possible for you to keep a 'decision diary'. Now, I do not for a minute suggest that you keep such a diary indefinitely. The best approach is to keep it for a few weeks, then leave it aside, maybe keeping it for another few weeks in a year or so's time. Keeping a decision diary for a limited period will speed up the process of your learning to be a more effective decision-maker, and so the small investment of time you make to keep one is repaid in time that might have been wasted as a consequence of bad decisions.

A decision diary is like an ordinary diary, except that the notes you make in it are to do with decisions you have thought about over the period. You may find that, rather than keep a special diary just for decisions, you start to jot down notes about your decisions in your ordinary diary. This is a good idea, because it's easier to manage just one diary than two or more and also because it puts decision-making where it should be—at the centre of things. Also, if notes about decisions are found next to notes about meetings, shopping, and so on, then you are more likely to treat your decisions in the same confident, straight-forward and business-like way that you treat these other aspects of your life.

You can write as much or as little about your decisions as you like, but I would suggest as a minimum the following entries:

1. The date on which the need to make the decision first became evident.
2. The date you finally made the decision, and what you decided.
3. The confidence with which you made the decision.
4. Any subsequent events or feelings throwing light on how good or bad your decision was.
5. Why you think it was a good/bad/indifferent decision.

It is probably not necessary to write much more than this because these entries will jog your memory concerning other relevant facts and details when you read them subsequently.

An example month from such a diary is shown on page 100. Each entry on the page has a 'decision number' by it, in this case between D2 and D12. This relates all the events concerned with a single decision. It is possible to trace the story of a decision, say D10, all the way through. Just keeping the diary encourages you to reflect and learn from past decisions. It can, in addition, be put

1st Feb	Sun	
2nd	Mon	
3rd	Tues	D9 At last I'm enjoying the new job. Pete was right after all.
4th	Wed	
5th	Thur	D10 Trixie died. Shall we get another dog?
6th	Fri	
7th	Sat	D7 I don't think Mum is happy. Should never have advised her to sell the house. Should have waited.
8th	Sun	
9th	Mon	D11 Jason wants to give up RK O-Level.
10th	Tues	
11th	Wed	D11 Heavy pressure from Jason.
12th	Thur	
13th	Fri	
14th	Sat	D2 Latest news on Vicky—life in Switzerland is wonderful. D4 Letter from accountant. Thank God we didn't sell those shares! I guess I just refused to be panicked.
15th	Sun	
16th	Mon	D12 Shall we take Mum on holiday with us this year?
17th	Tues	D5 Pete decided to take out private health insurance. I'm very anti.
18th	Wed	D12 Big family discussion. Mum is to come on holiday with us.
19th	Thur	
20th	Fri	D11 Told Jason he's got to stick it out. I'm sure it won't hurt him.
21st	Sat	
22nd	Sun	
23rd	Mon	D10 Can't stand life without a dog. Going to see puppies on Sat. Probably a mistake.
24th	Tues	
25th	Wed	D2 Pete's car broken down *again*. Why didn't we listen to Steve?!!
26th	Thur	
27th	Fri	
28th	Sat	D10 Bought new puppy. Jason doesn't like it.

A month from a decision diary

to more formal uses. It can help you to notice patterns behind good and bad decisions.

You can make a list of all the bad decisions made over the period. Look for common factors. Were a lot of them made in a hurry? Were you over-influenced by other people? Were you pig-headed in most of them and determined to go your own way? Do the same for the decisions you are pleased with. This book outlines a general approach to effective decision-making. There will also be particular strategies personal to you which improve your own decision-making. I have found, for example, that there is one friend I always consult when I feel I am about to make the wrong decision. Now, as soon as I feel the urge to telephone her, I ask myself what decision I am about to make and what is wrong with it. You may notice from the pattern in your decision diary that decisions you make at weekends are better than those you make during the week, or vice versa. The decision diary is the chance for you to discover all kinds of surprising things about yourself as a decision-maker.

A decision diary is also useful by reminding you of decision deadlines and time-limits (see Chapter Nine) which you have attached to particular decisions.

Reflect, but don't regret

The aim of the decision diary, and more generally of thinking about past decisions in whatever way suits you best, is not remorse or recrimination but self-awareness. Clearly we can all judge better with hindsight and we could all waste our lives with 'if only's. When we look back at decisions we made in the past, we begin to see how they shaped our lives and we are conscious of how differently we would have decided had we known then what we know now. It is tempting then to be drawn into regret, into wishing for what might have been. We may even blame ourselves for being so stupid or cowardly; we may blame others because they did not advise us better.

All such feelings are destructive. Rather than contributing to effective future decision-making, they stultify us with fear and bitterness. We need to reflect on our past decisions not so much in an emotional as in a scientific frame of mind. The decision diary can help us to put a little distance between ourselves and the decisions, which is useful: the decisions are objects of study, and we are to some extent detached from them. We must be generous to ourselves and understand that we made the best decisions we could at the time. What we are aiming to do now is understand why these were the best decisions we could make then so that we know what to change so as to be able to make better decisions in the future.

To clarify the difference between the two ways of looking at past decisions, we shall return to an earlier example. In Chapter Three, Alan Carpenter's story was told—he attempted a reconciliation with his wife after she had left him for another man. The reconciliation failed, so in one sense he had made a serious mistake in deciding to attempt it. He would have saved time, emotional energy, money and self-esteem, among other things, if he had been resolute and gone through with the divorce immediately.

How is Alan Carpenter then to look at this decision of his, to attempt a reconciliation? He could regret it, feel bitter, and contemplate how much easier his life would be now if only he had decided differently. He could forget about it as quickly as possible and move on. What I am advocating here is neither of these two courses of action. Alan can learn some useful things about his own decision-making from this past decision. He should ask himself why precisely he had to have a second go at his marriage. He should consider what advice he had and how he responded to it. Then, having taken what he can from the experience, he should be positive about that decision. True, it may not have been 'right' in the sense that he was hoping for an outcome which didn't in the event happen. But he has gained things from that decision, none the less. Most important of all, he has gained a certainty, which he didn't have before, that he must put that marriage behind him.

Conducting post-mortems on decisions without becoming morbid is difficult. But it is essential if we are to learn from the past.

Learn, or repeat the same mistakes

George Santayana wrote at the beginning of this century:

Progress, far from consisting in change, depends on retentive-
ness. . . . Those who cannot remember the past are con-
demned to repeat it.

This paradox, that we can only move on by looking back,
contains the most compelling argument for studying our past
decisions. Our effectiveness as decision-makers is hampered by
deep-seated fears, and habits of avoidance. Unless we examine
how we have been hampered in the past, we shall go on being
hampered in the same way in every decision we make.

An analogy is that of losing your way. Suppose you are driving
home from a strange place. You get lost, and find yourself back
where you were half an hour ago. Unless you can remember
something of the route you just took, you will probably continue
to go round in circles. You must force yourself to remember the
turnings you take so that if they are wrong you can be sure of
taking different ones next time. Of course, one of the things
which makes it difficult to note all the turnings is that you want to
believe they are right and that you will not have to try again. So it
is with decisions. We hope that we will get it absolutely right first
time, so we persuade ourselves that recording the steps is
unnecessary.

Putting decisions in perspective

Often we only understand the real reasons for our decisions
when we are at some distance from them in time. Suddenly,
looking back, we see that we always decided to do the opposite of
what our father suggested, or the same as our best friend, or took
the most financially rewarding course of action. Alternatively we
reflect on a particular decision, and can understand what was
really going on then. This is another good reason to reflect on
past decisions, and not only on recent ones but on decisions
which we made years ago. It can be very satisfying to understand
your own motives properly, and understanding is the first step to
control.

Decisions about having children are good ones to examine
from a distance. Often only when our children are safely into
adolescence can we look back to the time we conceived them and

face up to why. We may be able to acknowledge that we had them for very bad reasons, such as to make more claims on another adult, or to be able to stop working with a clear conscience, or as company because we were lonely. It may be safe to understand these things now, because we are now confident that we love our children for themselves despite their inauspicious beginnings.

You may wonder what the point is in calling to mind such ancient decisions, particularly when you are never likely to make the same decision again. Wouldn't it be better to leave the past alone?

The point is that the past will not leave us alone. Either we must be in charge of it or it will rule us. Guilt, shame, fear and resentment derive from choices in the past which we have never examined. By bringing the choices out into the light, we confront the emotions they still arouse in us, and can begin to control them.